A Monk in the Inner City

A MONK IN THE INNER CITY

THE ABCs OF A SPIRITUAL JOURNEY

Mary Lou Kownacki

ORBIS BOOKS

Maryknoll, New York 10545

Third Printing, September 2009

Founded in 1970, Orbis Books endeavors to publish works that enlighten the mind, nourish the spirit, and challenge the conscience. The publishing arm of the Maryknoll Fathers and Brothers, Orbis seeks to explore the global dimensions of the Christian faith and mission, to invite dialogue with diverse cultures and religious traditions, and to serve the cause of reconciliation and peace. The books published reflect the views of their authors and do not represent the official position of the Maryknoll Society. To learn more about Maryknoll and Orbis Books, please visit our website at www.maryknoll.org.

Published by Orbis Books, Maryknoll, NY 10545–0308.

Acknowledgment is gratefully made to *Commonweal, Praying Magazine, The Other Side, Fellowship Magazine, National Catholic Reporter, Sisters Today*, in which passages from this book have previously appeared, as well as publications by Pax Christi USA.

Manufactured in the United States of America.
Manuscript editing and typesetting by Joan Weber Laflamme.

Library of Congress Cataloging-in-Publication Data

Kownacki, Mary Lou.
   A monk in the inner city : the ABCs of a spiritual journey / Mary Lou Kownacki.
      p. cm.
   ISBN-13: 978–1–57075–760–0
   1. Church work with the poor—Catholic Church. 2. Church work—Pennsylvania—Erie. 3. Erie (Pa.)—Religious life and customs. 4. Kownacki, Mary Lou. 5. Benedictine nuns. 6. Monastic and religious life of women. I. Title.
   BX2347.8.P66K69 2008
   271'.97—dc22

                                                                 2007043308

Contents

𝓔

𝓕

𝓖

𝓗

𝓘

ℐ

𝒦

ℒ

ℳ

𝒩

𝒪

$\mathcal{P}$

$\mathcal{Q}$

$\mathcal{R}$

$\mathcal{S}$

$\mathcal{T}$

$\mathcal{U}$

$\mathcal{V}$

$\mathcal{W}$

$\mathcal{X}$

$\mathcal{Y}$

$\mathcal{Z}$

Introduction

"There are two ways to go through life," wrote psychologist and holocaust survivor Victor Frankl. "One is to gaze with fear and sadness at our wall calendar as each day we tear from it another sheet, noting that it grows thinner with each passing day. Another is to remove each successive leaf from the calendar, jot down a few diary notes on the back, and file it neatly and carefully away with its predecessors."

Those who keep a record, Frankl tells us, can reflect with pride and joy on all the life they have already lived to the full. What does it matter if they notice that they are growing old? What reason do they have to envy a young person—for possibilities for the future that awaits them? "No, thank you," they will say. "Instead of possibilities, I have realities in my past, not only the reality of work done and of love loved, but of suffering suffered. These are the things of which I am most proud."

I learned this lesson at the age of nineteen from Sister Theophane, my scholastic director. She discovered my love for books and writing and called me into her office. She showed me stacks of note cards on which she had recorded the title of every book she had read. I guess she was in her sixties then, so it was quite a stack. Each card contained the title of one book, a three-sentence synopsis of the plot, and her personal feelings about the story or ideas. "You might want to think about doing something like this," she said and dismissed me.

It was enough. I was taken with the notion of keeping a record of my life, devoted to what Gandhi called an "experiment in truth." My calendar notes chronicle my stumbling attempts to remain true to my call as a monk: to seek God by remaining rooted in community.

Anchored in the inner city of Erie, Pennsylvania, for forty years, I have been part of an ever-widening circle of communities—the Benedictine Sisters of Erie; the poor in the inner city; the peace movement; the monastic family in Africa, Asia, and Latin America; the people of Haiti; and the abandoned children of the world, always the children.

I have always leaned toward praxis rather than theory, and I believe that the purpose of monastic life is to embody Gandhi's advice to "be the change you want to see in the world." For almost all of my adult life, I have experimented with bringing this monastic vision to inner-city neighborhoods. Is it possible to be a visible sign that strangers can live together in God's love? How can we form hearts wide enough to welcome the traveler, the outcast, and the neighbor? If *listen* is the compass point of Saint Benedict's Rule, what happens if we listen to and learn from the people we serve, especially the poorest? How do the values of monastic stewardship, dignified human labor, sacred leisure, and reverence for all living things affect the forgotten faces of our society? It is my hope that in these new wastelands, in the midst of the marginalized of the earth, in the living of these questions a new monasticism will be born.

All through the years I have kept notes on the back of my calendar pages, reflections about the people and events that touched and transformed my heart. "I must write it all out, at any cost. Writing is thinking. It is more than living, for it is being conscious of living," wrote Anne Morrow Lindbergh. And so I wrote. And wrote.

I once read that an ABC book is a Polish genre, a literary form loosely composed of short, alphabetically arranged entries. With a bow to the ancestors, I follow their form here.

Come, then. This monk invites you into her inner-city home. Let me pour you a drink while I show you my stack of note cards—a synopsis of a life. "You might want to think about doing something like this."

I stay because I long to become the monk that Ryokan described, "Oh, that my monk's robes were wide enough to embrace the suffering world."

THE $\mathcal{ABC}$s
of a
SPIRITUAL JOURNEY

Abandoned places

No alarm awakens me at 5 a.m., just habit. In the dark I kiss my rosary and put it on the nightstand. All is quiet. I sit. Only candlelight and an icon of the Black Madonna. "Mercy, mercy, mercy," I pray. Let the mercy of God rain down. Mercy on the corner bar. Mercy on the crack house down the street. Mercy on the prostitute coming home with money to feed her children. Mercy on the children sleeping through a winter storm, rags stuffed in their bedroom windows. Mercy, mercy, mercy.

I live as a monk in a neighborhood that people are afraid to drive through, let alone visit. I like to think of myself as one of a long line of monks like Ryokan or Basho or Syncletica or Lao Tsu or Antony, those eccentrics who took to the loneliness to meet their God.

Besides lacking a certain purity of soul that I so admire in these desert and mountain recluses, I also live in the midst of an inner city. It is here, in a place that the late Trappist monk Thomas Merton called the new wilderness, that I built my hut.

Merton thought it the new desert because the centers of our cities are barren and dry, devoid of hope, of promise, of possibility. Demons dwell in the boarded-up houses, the dark alleys, the abandoned storefronts, and they attack as soon as the sun sets. The demons come with promises of nirvana in powder and capsules and sex, and they have their way, roaming the streets at will.

As in all deserts, there is a starkness that attracts and appeals. There is no pretension here. Everything is stripped bare. The homes have no fancy facades. No fresh paint. No new siding. No screen doors. The windows have no curtains. There are no flowers, not even grass in most yards, back or front. It is a visual of what John of the Cross called "the dark night of the soul." Everything down to bare necessity and no comfort in sight.

The people are naked, too. "I'm on the drugs," Miss Cynthia tells me after she finishes shoveling my walk. Clifton beats his breast for years of alcohol and cocaine and a wasted life. Miss Ruby weeps over her son. No bravado, no false fronts, no masks.

But in the "dark night" is great beauty and goodness, if you stay awake to it. I wonder at the simple acts of goodness that I witness each day in circumstances where cactus, not orchids, should grow.

Take my neighbor Mr. Johnson, who struggles to raise a family of nine children. He has a bad heart and gets by on part-time paving jobs, but just barely. One evening Mr. Johnson brought out his grill and filled the summer air with barbecued ribs, chicken, and hot dogs. And he gave them away free, along with potato salad, deviled eggs, and baked beans. He gave them away free to dozens of children who flocked to his house and to every adult who lived on the block or happened to be walking by.

Talk about taking the world into your arms. Here was a poor man giving of his sustenance. Here was the widow's mite enfleshed before my eyes. Here was Mr. Johnson, a reminder of a God who gives freely, without measure, and with overflowing extravagance.

What do I do here? I play. I teach. I find myself wide-eyed with tenderness toward the children. When I first moved back to my childhood home, there were thirty-four children living on this one city block. Thirty-four children to play with, to read to, to treat with candy.

We started a self-help program called One Block at a Time. Thanks to small grants and donations, the children could earn hand-printed dollars, only redeemable at a neighborhood grocery store, if they participated in a daily cleanup of the block. And volunteers helped with a summer reading program that culminated in a picnic and party at an indoor water park. We spent two wonderful years together. In the third year every child, except one, moved out. Thirty-three children left.

Why did they move? Well, it had something to do with my six-year-old neighbor being molested by the little boys in the block. It had something to do with seven abandoned houses in the block. That means abandoned backyards with abandoned sheds where little boys take little girls to "hump" them.

It had something to do with gangs gathering in front of the abandoned houses to roll craps all night long.

It had something to do with an eleven-year-old girl being raped in the corner crack house and then forced to walk home half naked. "She was willin'," the teenagers told the cops. "She was willin'."

Wouldn't you move if you were a mother with children? Is it hopeless? I refuse to surrender.

My refrigerator is covered with letters from the children. "Yuz is a life-saver," one writes. Another explains, "i be bad but that going to change."

When my Aunt Verna died, her funeral liturgy was in the neighborhood church. As we were leaving the church behind the casket, I could see Jimanji standing on the sidewalk. When I saw him, I had two thoughts: isn't it nice that one of the neighborhood children came to see my aunt being buried, and I hope this child doesn't do or say something that will be interpreted as disrespectful and open the racist bag. Then I exited the church and saw ten neighborhood children, all standing quietly and respectfully, looking at me with great attention. I'd never seen them so well behaved as a group. A few parishioners were doing some minor landscaping and one of them, Bob, asked the children why they had gone to church. "We heard Miss Kownacki's aunt died, and we went to show our respect and honor."

But mostly I hold on to Corey's choice. I celebrated Corey's birthday, as I did all the children's birthdays, by taking him to a book store and having him choose a book. Ten-year-old Corey chose an illustrated version of Robert Frost's poem "Stopping by Woods on a Snowy Evening." He memorized a stanza, and he recites it every time he comes to my house for a visit:

> The woods are lovely, dark and deep,
> But I have promises to keep,
> And miles to go before I sleep,
> And miles to go before I sleep.

Don't talk to me about the death of hope.

What do I do here? I listen. I get to know my neighbors, really know them. I listen to their hopes and dreams for decent jobs, decent homes, a safe place to raise their children. They are worried about their children, especially their teenagers, who can see no future except minimum-paying jobs, lockup, or dropping out to the streets.

What do I do here? I plead a case for presence, beauty, community, and a call to follow God into the wilderness.

Once upon a time men and women who wanted to seek God relocated themselves in abandoned places. These "wilderness places," often associated with the desert, gave the seekers a unique perspective and freedom.

Living on the margins of society, stripped of the trappings of social expectation and pressure, they began to see differently. Immersed in the word of God, they began to listen differently. They put on the broken heart of God and spoke the truth on God's behalf for the poor, the victims of injustice, the suffering.

Their location in the wilderness gave them great freedom. Why? Because no one paid attention to them. Because they were not the movers and shakers of the city. Because they had no political influence, no one cared what they did. No one even noticed their quiet works of transformation among the poor until suddenly "the desert and parched land bloomed with abundant flowers."

In my hometown there are a number of "God seekers" who have relocated to the inner city. They are quietly praying and working and building small communities "in the shell of the old." I am part of one such group—married couples, single men and women, sisters—interested in the Rule of Saint Benedict. We have started to meet in the hope of forming another spiritually intense center that can have an influential presence in the area.

Our goals are modest: to plant daffodils, to rebuild abandoned homes, to paint porches, to read to children, to pray together, to grow vegetables, to become a neighborhood, a community. Nothing spectacular, just a snippet of "the kingdom of God, come on earth as it is in heaven."

What do I do here? I write. Each morning I sit down in my storefront study and write a short poem. I write about family. About my mother taken so suddenly so many years ago. About my dad, who died as he always hoped—in his home cared for by loved ones. I write about lost love and nature and inner wars. But mostly I write about this block and the children whose lives have become intertwined with mine. I write about reclaiming the sense of possibility I myself knew on this street as a child:

> Come, children, let us scatter
> flower seeds in the neighborhood
> of no lawns or birds.
> Let us turn one small street
> into a greenhouse
> of the possible.

I write about days when spiritual security, not fear, was a neighborhood's gift to children:

> At least twice a day
> century-old church bells remind
> that children once played in this street
> without pet Rottweilers
> tied to lampposts.

I write about the sin of ignoring those who have the same needs we all do but no way to satisfy them:

> Poor people on my street
> rummaging through city trash
> for stained mattresses, torn chairs
> a chipped vase
> to hold a stolen daffodil.

It is one way of trying to stretch my monk's robe until, like Ryokan's, it embraces the suffering world.

Angels

I've had two life-changing encounters with angels. When I was sixteen an angel appeared to me. Granted, I had just snuck into the house after a Friday night illegal beer party. But there it was, right in the corner of my bedroom, all aglow.

I wasn't frightened, only embarrassed about drinking so much. "I'm making a real mess of my life," I told the angel. "What should I do?"

"You'd better go to the convent," the angel replied.

"Are you sure?" I asked. "I'm really not the type."

"I'm positive," the angel said.

"Okay," I answered. And that was it.

The next day I told my mother I was entering the convent and went to the *Book of Saints* to pick out my future sister's name (Sebastian, patron of athletes and soldiers, is what I chose. I was very patriotic then, and I was an excellent athlete.) The next Monday I joined the vocation club, and the following year I entered the Benedictine Sisters of Erie.

To this day I'm not sure whether the angel was the result of too much beer, a dream, or an actual visit. Whatever, it changed my life.

The second encounter came when I visited the angel tree at the Metropolitan Museum of Art in New York City one Christmas season. I was studying in New York, and this was my first visit to the museum. On a Sunday afternoon in mid-December it was jammed, and I just followed the crowd into a very large room. Suddenly all the holiday noise, talk, and bustle stopped, and a great silence filled the vast hall. The crowd of holiday visitors was hushed, gazing reverently at the largest Christmas tree I had ever seen. And the most breathtaking. It front of me was a thirty-foot blue spruce covered with elegant, hand-sculptured angels. How to describe them? How to capture the divine aura, the radiance, the obvious mystical rapture? The fifty or so angels seemed in flight, their hair waving wildly as if caught in a strong wind. Many were swinging silver-gilt censors; some were just poised in adoration. All were turned toward the tiny child in the crib, almost invisible at the foot of the tree. Under the tree, magi, shepherds, animals, townspeople, and travelers representing every corner of the earth hurried toward the manger, about two hundred figurines in all.

But it was the angels that sent me to the celestial sphere. The faces of the angels, all aglow with awe and wonder and mystery! It was a tender and terrible scene; for a moment I was suspended between heaven and earth.

And then the music began. "O Holy Night" poured out of the loudspeaker and bathed the hall with heavenly song. Truly I heard the angels sing. All I wanted to do was to prostrate myself and adore.

Abraham Maslow would call my moment a peak experience; monastics might speak of a contemplative moment. I have returned to the angel tree at the Met two other times, and even though it is always a sacred moment, I haven't recaptured the peak experience of my first encounter.

Since the age of sixteen, then, I have been very fond of winged creatures bathed in light. I'm especially attracted to Christmas angels, and here's why.

One, angels are good for my dreams. It can be such a dull, predictable, boring world, can't it? All those rational managers in charge of everything. All those disciples of gray. Ah, but angels appearing to virgins and shepherds and magi, now that's a reason to get out of bed in the morning. If those angel visits are true, then anything is possible. I can dream dreams of no abused children, of beds for all the homeless, of food for all the hungry. Even world peace is possible.

Two, angels teach me how to pray. Just listen to their prayer on Christmas night, "Glory to God in the highest." No self-preoccupation here, only praise and more praise. No gloom and doom here, just song and celebration. "Peace on earth," the angels proclaim. What a wonderful blessing to shower on our world. What a way to proclaim that all earth is holy ground. "To pray without ceasing," the angels tell me, "is to hold both God and the world in my heart while chanting 'holy, holy, holy.'"

Three, angels fill me with holy terror. Or maybe it is heart-breaking beauty and soul-stripping truth. Remember, at the sight of the angels the shepherds were filled with both fear and immeasurable joy. That's why I'm not crazy about cute, plump, cherub angels. I like pictures and statues of wild-looking ones, hair blowing in the wind, incense holders swinging wildly. "Who can see the face of God and live?" Moses asked. Well, angels have. What I see in the faces of these angels is the price paid for daring to enter the holy presence, and I am forced to my knees.

Four, angels fill me with courage. "Every blade of grass has an angel over it saying, 'Grow,'" the Talmud reads. With an angel of God protecting me, I have no excuse for not imitating the shepherds and carrying God's message to the country-side. I can speak out against injustice. I can risk welcoming strangers. I can even face myself in the mirror.

Five, angels call me to my better self. Because of an angel's call, Mary risked her reputation and became "blessed among women." Because of an angel's call, Joseph risked ridicule and brought hope to the world. Because of an angel's call, the shepherds faced their fears and raced toward a star in the night. I want to run, heart overflowing, into the heart of God, too. But apathy often wins out, and I settle for being less than I am.

Six, angels tell me something about God. As Meister Eckhart wrote, "That's all an angel is, an idea of God." The main insight into God that I've learned from angels is to pay attention to the poor. The first to know about the birth of Jesus were the shepherds, the soup-kitchen clients of Bethlehem. And in scripture, angels often come to earth disguised as strangers.

We can never prove it, but we think Alfred A. was an angel. He appeared at our soup kitchen one day in the image of a Native American—tall, dark skin, high cheekbones, jet-black hair pulled back in a ponytail. After eating a meal, he walked up to the serving counter and asked for a table napkin. Then he took a pencil from his vest pocket, stood at the counter, and began to scribble on the napkin.

A few minutes later he handed one of the volunteers the paper napkin and said, "I feel the presence of God here." On the napkin was a sketch of the face of Jesus. Then he walked out the door, and we haven't seen him since. The only proof we have that he appeared is that sketch and the signature, Alfred A.

What message from God did we get from our disguised angel? I think Alfred A. reminded us that to serve the stranger, the poor, is an act of worship. Whenever we treat the stranger with respect, with kindness, with unconditional love, we worship God.

If we get only one message from an angel in our lifetime, may it be the one delivered by Alfred Angel: "I feel the presence of God here."

Anniversaries

To prepare materials for the twentieth anniversary of the soup kitchen, I spent a few hours looking through old photos, slides, and news clippings. When I finished, all I could think of was the parable of the barren fig tree. In that story Jesus talks about a man who wanted to cut down a fig tree because it had not borne fruit since it was planted. But the gardener tells him, "Let it alone for one more year, until I dig around it and put some manure on it."

Like the fig tree, there's no fruit at the soup kitchen. All we have after thirty years are the same faces, older now and wearier after two decades of standing in line for a daily meal. We also have growing numbers of hungry.

Oh, now and then we get a "bud." A few days ago Sister Miller, director of Emmaus, was in a store when a man approached her. "Excuse me," he said, "but you're Sister Mary, right? Two years ago I lost my job and my mother died. I was depressed, broke, and forced to go to the soup kitchen. You have no idea what it was like for me to stand in line for food. Since then things have picked up. I'm a baker here, and I want to give you a donation." As I said, a tiny, tiny bud.

The temptation is to cut down the fig tree. Close the soup kitchen and admit defeat. We can never change the system by feeding its victims. But the parable of the fig tree won't let us do that. It insists that we continue to choose life by nurturing a seemingly dead fig tree. Why? Because whether it bears figs is not up to us, but preparing the soil *is* possible. If and when and where the fig tree blossoms is God's business.

The question is not whether the soup kitchen has changed things, made a difference, brought justice to the city's poor. The real question is: have we changed? After thirty years have we become kinder, more merciful, less judgmental? Do we continue feeding the poor because we want to see the fruits of our efforts? Or do we continue serving soup because we love? And do we love enough not to give up on anything or anyone? Least of all, a barren fig tree.

(I'm not fooled by the gardener's threat to cut down the tree in a year if it doesn't bear fruit. I know how God counts time. "A thousand years in your sight are as yesterday that is past," Psalm 90 reads. According to those calculations the barren fig tree has more than a few centuries left.)

Bearing Witness

The torso of a young man was found in a trash bin, his two legs sawed off. He had been stabbed ten times, six times in the right side of his face and four times in the upper chest. His legs were found nearby, wrapped in a plastic trash bag.

All murders are shocking. But this one was particularly gruesome, especially for a city like Erie that still prides itself on having a small hometown touch.

Every time a murder occurs in Erie, our sisters gather at the crime site and hold a prayer service. So, three days after the body was discovered, we joined in song and scripture near the train station. During the prayer Sister Ann and Sister Lynn told us about their visit with the victim's father the day before. "We took a loaf of Sister Irene's bread, and he was so touched by that simple gift," Sister Ann said. She talked about how bewildered the father was, wondering why anyone would do such a thing to his son. "We prayed with him and tried to be present to his suffering," she continued. "He was so grateful that we had come bearing bread and words of comfort."

I came to the service feeling numb; this killing was too much for me to stomach. Nothing, I thought, can slow down the escalating violence overtaking our culture. So I was surprised when the tears slid down my face, but I knew what my body was telling me—this was the first time I had really prayed in a long, long time. The sisters who broke bread with the victim's family and the remnant gathered on the street corner were "bearing witness." I was "bearing witness." And to bear witness is a profound expression of eucharist. To be present to suffering, just present, without pretending to have answers, is how we most radically follow Jesus' invitation: "remember me."

This is the real presence that can lead to healing, to reconciliation, to peace.

Beauty

I listen to someone playing a piano in one of the rotting apartments that abut my home. Believe me, the sweet melody pouring in my open windows on a Saturday morning, thirty minutes of beauty overtaking poverty, is balm enough momentarily to heal the wounded city. Note upon note is reason enough to stay, reason enough to stake your life on Dostoyevsky's prediction: In the end beauty will save the world.

"What's happening there?" one of the children asked when they saw the bulldozers.

"They're putting up another large drugstore and knocking down all the buildings on the corner," I explained to the four children I was driving home from the Art House, an after-school program where I teach poetry.

"Not that beautiful building," one of the children exclaimed.

"Yes," I said, "the old bank building is going."

"Why?" another asked. "It's my favorite building."

All four children were upset. They called the old Bank of Erie beautiful and didn't understand why someone would choose to destroy that impressive structure, especially since it was surrounded by blocks of deteriorating, ugly buildings.

None of the children in the car had any history with that building. None of their grandparents or parents came from eastside Erie. What they had in common was this: they had recently immigrated to this country and fallen in love with the old bank building.

The children's unsolicited and genuine feelings of sadness and outrage both surprised and provoked me. Is a feel for beauty that instinctive in children, I wondered. Or was it a matter of contrast, that in this part of town there is so little left to comfort the eye that a grand old building automatically attracts?

I wondered, too, if the stone structure didn't speak to their subconscious of stability, of something that will last beyond the architecturally boring fast-food places and chain stores that dot their landscapes.

Mostly, though, the children made me angry with myself for not doing anything to stop the city from allowing the destruction of this historical treasure. For me, swinging the wrecking ball is like injecting a revered and venerable grandparent with strychnine. The old bank, built in 1917, provided a visual reminder that at one time this part of the city was a main street of thriving businesses, family recreation, open markets, and neighbors that cared for one another—and that it can be that again.

My only solace is that constant exposure to the beautiful at the Art House is making a dent in the lives of children. If the children in my car learned to recognize the beautiful and desired to preserve it, maybe their generation will not destroy a thing of beauty for profit disguised as progress.

A Beginner's Mind

What the world needs now is a beginner's mind. *Beginner's mind* is a Zen term that roughly means being open to all ideas, to all people, to all experiences.

I do not have a beginner's mind, but I find it both inviting and desirable when I recognize it in another. I would like to possess that childlike wonder that is free of prejudice and judgment and is open to the present moment.

Lack of a beginner's mind can be found in this story: A medieval Irish monk died and was buried in the monastery wall, as was the custom. One day the monks heard a song coming from within the wall and removed the stones to find their brother alive and well. He began to tell them what he had learned in his journey beyond—and everything was contrary to the teachings of the church. So the brothers put him back in the wall and sealed the crypt forever.

Gandhi had a beginner's mind. He looked upon his practice of nonviolence as a search for Truth. Gandhi maintained that if we are serious about finding Truth, we cannot harm another person, especially if that person disagrees with us. Why? Because in killing our enemy, we destroy a part of the Truth that we do not have. Gandhi liked to say: "There is my truth. There is your truth. There is *the* Truth."

I admit to walking like someone barefoot on crushed glass when it comes to discussing truth. I walk very gingerly. It is tempting to spew out answers with the certainty of the Godhead. The government, for example, is certain that the way to peace is through war. That the way to stop terrorism is to rain down terror on innocent women and children. That the way to stop murder is to murder those who commit murder. My faith tradition, the Roman Catholic Church, has volumes of certainties. For example, women can never be ordained, and lesbians and gays can never express physical intimacy.

Rather than pronouncement, proof text, and dogma, I prefer to enter the discussion on truth through stories. Thich Nhat Hanh, the best-selling Buddhist author and one of the great spiritual figures of our time, is the source of one of my favorites:

> One day a father left his village on business, and while he was gone bandits came and burned down the village and kidnapped his son. When the father returned, he found a burned corpse near his home and thought it was the remains of his son. The father almost went mad with grief and after an elaborate cremation ceremony placed the ashes of his son in a beautiful velvet bag, which he carried with him always.
>
> One day his son escaped from his kidnappers and arrived at his father's home at midnight. He knocked, and his father, who was holding the velvet bag, said, "Who's there?" The child answered: "It's me, Papa. Open the

door. It's your son." But the father was so certain that his son was dead that he told the boy to stop tormenting him and to go away. The boy knocked and knocked, but the father never answered. He just held the velvet bag closer and cried without ceasing. Finally, the child left, and the father and son never saw one another.

Every time I find myself hotly defending a cherished belief, I remember this story. Every time I find myself shouting my truth at an opposing idea, as if the volume of my defense makes it truer, I check for the velvet bag. Every time I refuse to read or listen to an opposing view, every time I mock or belittle another's truth, I become the father who has lost a beginner's mind.

"In the beginner's mind there are many possibilities, in the expert's there are few," wrote Shunryu Suzuki. I try to remember that when I listen to *Crossfire*, to a presidential speech, or to the latest official document from the pulpit.

C

Children

Our inner-city landscape is littered with writhing children. They are rolling in pain, dying in spirit from hunger, neglect, and abuse.

A boy dropped in after school and asked, "Can I draw somewhere?" Even though our community's new Inner-City Neighborhood Art House wasn't officially open, the sister in charge led the boy to an easel—he was our first student. The twelve year old drew a picture of a boy and then scribbled lines through the drawing with a black marker. The sister made no comment about the picture but said simply: "All artists give titles to their pictures. Do you have a title for your drawing?" The boy thought a moment and asked, "How do you spell *soul*?" The sister told him. He then titled his picture "The Lost Soul."

Recently a mother asked my friend, Sister Mary, for special prayers. Her five year old had attempted suicide over the weekend, slitting her wrist. Her five year old.

A nine-year-old girl I know goes home every day after school and is alone until 10:30 p.m. when her single mother returns from work.

Children who attended our Kids' Cafe this summer received a breakfast and a lunch. "What will you have for supper this evening?" one of our sisters asked a child as he was returning his emptied dishes. "What's supper?" he asked. "We only eat in school." Children in this program didn't recognize hard-cooked eggs. Very few had ever eaten a fresh orange.

When I think of toys for children, Barbie dolls, video games, and remote-control trucks come to mind. That's why Angel and her sister, Michelle, came as such a shock. These two little girls play with roaches. "There are so many at my grandma's house," Angel told us. "We don't catch mama and papa roaches 'cause they bite," she explained. "But we catch the little babies and let them run up and down our hands and we name them. I call mine Angel 1 and Angel 2 and. . . . "

Often I am awakened from sleep by the sound of children's voices on the street. It is not unusual for my alarm clock to be showing one or two in the morning. What are seven year olds and eleven year olds doing out on cruel inner-city streets at this hour?

In my poetry class at the Neighborhood Art House I asked the children to write lines beginning with, "I remember. . . . " One remembered watching while a stray pit bull entered her house and tore her cat to shreds and being unable to help. Another remembered playing with a friend who was abducted right before her eyes. A third wrote about someone breaking into her house and putting a gun to her head. A fourth remembered waiting all day on her birthday for her father to take her fishing as he had promised and watching him stagger up the front steps late at night.

Armies of children wandering a wasteland of hunger, broken dreams, and living nightmares. What can we do?

The short story "Soul Murder" by David Mamet gives us a clue. In the story a man witnesses a mother being cruel to one of her little boys, belittling him in a public place and punishing him further by refusing to let him go to the bathroom. The little boy sits on a bench, puts his head down on his knees, presses his hands over his ears, and rocks back and forth. When the mother goes to the restroom, the man imagines himself walking up to the little boy, sitting beside him, and whispering: "I am your guardian angel. I have been sent to tell you this: you are not bad but good."

Then the man fantasizes that he gives the boy a quarter and tells him that it is magic. Whenever the boy sees or touches it he will magically remember that he is not bad but good. The man tells him that someday he will lose the coin, but that's part of the plan. When the coin is lost it means that any time the boy sees any coin he will remember that he is good. Then the man imagines walking away. As he finishes his fantasy, the man sees the woman rejoin the children, smiling at two of them and glaring at the one she had belittled. They all go off.

We can be alert for children who are battered by life and in need of some sign of love and hope. We can look for them in our inner-city playgrounds, soup kitchens, shelters, schools, suburban streets, and at our own dinner tables. When we find any "lost souls," we can whisper some word of comfort or give them a magic gift that lets them know they are good.

Christmas

What is the meaning of Christmas? Whenever this question rises in me, I remember a story I read by Susan Griffin, who heard it from Odette, a holocaust survivor:

A truck, crowded with concentration-camp victims, is on its way to the gas chambers. Everyone, including the guards, is silent, because all know the final destination. Suddenly a man grabs the hand of one of the condemned and begins to read his palm. "Oh, I see you have a long lifeline," he says aloud. "And you are going to have three children." He is filled with excitement and goes from one man to another predicting futures filled with long lives, loving families, and great joy. Suddenly the mood of the prisoners changes. One can sense a rising hope. Within moments the guards become confused—what seemed inevitable is now in doubt. For whatever reason— surprise, uncertainty, wonder—the men are taken back to the barracks instead of to the chambers.

The palm reader was the poet Robert Desnos. What the poet did for these passengers to Auschwitz was to revive the imaginations of those trapped by despair.

Christmas is the feast when God reinforces the poet's intuition and takes a chance on creative imagination.

When God enters human history as a poor child of a virgin, born in a stable with angels filling the sky, the old order is thrown into confusion. Who holds power now? How does the world look? How does it work? What holds it together? This shift in perspective provokes powerful changes. Anything becomes possible. It is possible that the powerless will dethrone the powerful. It is possible that swords will be beaten into plowshares. It is possible that a Berlin Wall can fall, that the poor will triumph, that slaves can be freed, that women can be ordained, that all who call earth home can live to fullness.

What is the meaning of Christmas? To imitate God and imagine a different world.

Community

When I lived in an intentional peace community, the Pax Center, a friend of ours brought a priest to a Wednesday evening liturgy and potluck supper. "He's very interested in peace and justice," our friend explained. "We were talking about radical Christian communities, and I told him Erie had one. So I brought him to meet you."

The visitor is polite but definitely apprehensive. All during liturgy he shifts uneasily in his chair and keeps glancing at the others gathered in the chapel; occasionally he looks toward the door.

I wonder what he is expecting. The first reading from *The Prison Letters of Fidel Castro* to the revolutionary cadres in northwestern Pennsylvania? A dialogue homily outlining a sophisticated strategy to end the arms race? The FBI suddenly appearing and arresting us for plotting a break-in to smash missile parts at the local GE plant? A cache of machine guns carried up during the offertory procession?

If I had any compassion, I would call him aside and explain. "Don't be frightened, Father." The person singing off key wouldn't know Bishop Gumbleton from Mao Tse Tung from Che Guevara; she spent most of her life in an institution for the mentally retarded. The young man sitting across from us with the wild look in his eyes is not a representative of the Latin American Revolutionary Front; he's an out-patient from Hamot Mental Health. The attractive woman on your right is a former prostitute and a rather successful shoplifter. Don't be disappointed, though. The elderly gentleman on your left will hand you leaflets as you leave the chapel. These leaflets will explain how you can become a slave of the Blessed Virgin Mary.

When the doorbell rings during the gospel reading, I notice that you jump. Expecting Dan Berrigan, perhaps? It's only Rose, our toilet-paper lady. She comes twice a week for toilet paper and five dollars. She uses the toilet paper for everything: washing and drying dishes, bathing, cleaning floors. She tells me that using toilet paper is more sanitary than using cloth towels. All last winter Rose and five cats lived in a broken-down car. Now she and the cats move from apartment to apartment, one step ahead of the rent collector. She pays for cat food and clothes by camping out on the front steps of the rectory until the pastor gets so embarrassed he slips her some money.

She calls daily begging for money and toilet paper. Did I mention the five dollars is used to buy cat food?

"You know the rules," I tell her. "Five dollars and four rolls of toilet paper. Unless, of course, you go to mental health. Then I'll try to help you with rent and food."

"Mental health," she screams into the receiver. "And you call yourself a sister? Anyone who lives at the Pax Center belongs in mental health."

She's probably right.

Did I notice your ears perk up, Father, when those strange footsteps started in the hall? Don't go home thinking the ghost of Dorothy Day roams our halls, blessing our work. That was my ninety-five-year-old uncle shuffling to the bathroom. Since he can barely walk, I don't know what we'll do with him when the revolution comes and we take to the streets.

The tired looking people in the chapel are the hub of Pax Center. No, the dark circles under their eyes didn't come from holding heavy political meetings into the night. All of them have ordinary full-time jobs and after an eight-hour work day, they begin Pax Center work: a shift at the soup kitchen, fix supper for fifteen, prepare for prayer, collate our newspaper, listen to the young woman the police brought in at midnight for shelter, clean a bathroom, attend an evening meeting. There's not much personal time or private space. Now and then you might find the Pax community in front of the Erie Federal Building or the White House protesting nuclear arms. But not too often. No time, even less energy.

After hearing this, the visitor might ask—this is a radical Christian community hoping to change the world?

And I would answer: "Well, Father, I can understand your confusion. It's not exactly what I had in mind ten years ago either. But I'm learning. All of us are."

Contemplative Vision

I attended a retreat on the spirituality of the earth led by Thomas Berry, a leading environmental theologian. "The problem with the environmental movement," he said, "is lack of depth." He explained that there is a lack of contemplation, of wisdom, of spirituality in the movement, a lack of mystics, if you will. And because of this lack, the changes we see in the environment are cosmetic, not the profound, soulful efforts needed to save the earth.

I compared his comments to my lifelong experiences in the peace movement and agreed with his "lack of depth" assessment. A movement that places its energy and hope on legislation, elections, and church statements is a superficial one—lots of frenetic, well-motivated action, but no soul-spirited center.

I blame this lack of spiritual depth on the monastic tradition in the church. Benedictine communities like mine issue
documents stating that we are stewards of the contemplative
vision. We claim that we are entrusted with soul shaping, with
forming the contemplative heart, with preparing that place of
love from which all action flows. "By their deeds you shall
know them," Jesus said when asked how you could tell the
fake from the true.

How would others know if we are true stewards of the contemplative vision? Easy. We would do outrageous things because love, not a political agenda, would impel us to act. We
would look upon the face of every man and woman and recognize a brother or sister. We would know the deer, the turtle,
the ant, the wind, the rain as part of the earth's family. We
would have such hospitality of heart that we would recognize
all creation and welcome it as the sacred community. And we
would take courageous and scandalous risks on behalf of love.
We would dance with poets and mystics and artists and clowns
in tribute to life, no matter the circumstances.

People would know that we had touched divine largesse,
abundance, and magnanimity because we would not tolerate
injustice or violence to any part of creation, because we would
"tear down the mighty from their thrones and lift up the down-
trodden." Yes, by our deeds they would know us as contem-
platives.

We would be the kind of lovers Dostoyevsky had in mind
when he wrote: "Love all of God's creation, the whole and
every grain of sand in it. Love every leaf, every ray of God's
light. Love the animals, love the plants, love everything. If
you love everything, you will perceive the divine mystery of
things." This is the contemplative vision so sorely needed. This
is the "depth of soul" that will change the earth.

Courage

A game of mumblety-peg taught me all I had to know about
the journey from fear to courage. How we got the jackknife, I

don't remember. Perhaps we all chipped in and bought it at the corner variety store. What I do remember is the neighborhood gang owning our first knife and having a great time playing mumblety-peg in front of my house. By neighborhood gang I mean all the boys in my neighborhood and me. You remember mumblety-peg? We didn't have a copy of *Hoyle's Rules of Games*, and so we played it this way. Touch the blade to your forehead—headsies—and flip it to the ground. If the knife didn't stick, the next kid gets a turn. If it does stick in the grass, you move it to your nose—nosie—and flip again. A few of us were at "elbows" when Joey suddenly grabbed the knife and ran home.

At ten, Joey was the oldest of the neighborhood gang, a year older than I, and the closest we had to a bully on the block. After a quick caucus, we decided to reclaim our knife and marched to Joey's house with me in the lead.

Joey was in the front yard playing, and when he refused to return the knife, all the kids started yelling, "Go get him, Mary Lou." What could I do? Joey had committed a wrong, stolen something from the weaker and less powerful. The wrong had to be righted, and I was the leader of the gang. Like the rest of the kids, I was afraid of Joey, but with my friends cheering me on I went at him swinging. In a minute he was on the ground and I was on top of him, fists pummeling his face. "Give us back our knife," I kept repeating. Next thing I knew his dad was pulling us apart and telling his son, "I told you never to pick on girls, Joey." We got our knife back.

In that childhood incident I began to discover that the journey from fear to courage had something to do with entering the good fight, no matter how frightened I was.

In later years, when I became part of the peace movement and began to question whether swinging fists was the best way to right a wrong, I came upon this quotation from Mahatma Gandhi: "Those who tremble and take to their heels the moment they see two people fighting are not nonviolent but cowards. The nonviolent will lay down their lives preventing such quarrels."

There was no getting off the hook. Entering the fight was still the criterion for the brave, the courageous, and now, the nonviolent heart.

Since Joey-the-knife-stealer, I've discovered there are many bullies on the block, many who take advantage of the weak and powerless. With knees shaking, I've tried to stand up to bullies in Vietnam, El Salvador, Iraq, Haiti, and the United States. But instead of using fists I've confronted with prayer, silent vigils, demonstrations, advocacy, and civil disobedience.

Every time I've entered the fray, I've had to confront my fears and get to know them better. When I helped monitor Haiti's first democratic election—the one that swept Jean-Bertrand Aristide into power—I had to confront my fear of personal injury or death and discover that the lives of the poor were more important to me than my own safety.

On the other hand, I stood on the sidelines not so long ago and watched two men in a street fight swing chains at one another and never intervened. Obviously I'm still afraid to die and deep down think my life is worth more than either of those two drunks. Gandhi's insight into the truly nonviolent heart is still at work in me.

So I thank God for Joey-the-knife-stealer. Every time I find myself being pushed into situations in which I have to confront a bully to try to right a wrong, I have a childhood mantra to help strengthen my trembling knees. If I listen hard enough, I can hear the voices of innocent and defenseless children everywhere chanting, "Go get him, Mary Lou. Go get him."

Cry of the Poor

The poor of Haiti sit on the street and sell hand-carved wooden bells with this engraved message: "No one can hear the sound of the wooden bell or the cry of the poor." To hear the cry of the poor, don't you have to go into their neighborhoods?

A couple of years ago a local elementary school was having a retreat, and part of the experience was to come into the inner city. A few parents protested—they were afraid to have their children come to the soup kitchen. They were right. To hear the cry of the poor can change your life—can change it forever.

DC Jail

The Secret Service guard puts the walkie-talkie to his mouth as we pass by: "The demonstrators are entering the White House." So it goes as we enter the tour line. It is almost a choreographed scenario: the police are told how many are going to demonstrate, the place we will kneel to pray, who the demonstrators are. No surprises, everything is in the open—very Gandhian civil disobedience.

Once we enter the White House driveway, the five of us from Erie step over the chain-link fence that marks the legal tour area and kneel down to pray. "We are here to demonstrate by our presence, before God, that we will not be silent as our country takes food from the hungry . . . for the purpose of building up our arsenals," our prayer begins. A dozen Secret Service police surround us, fence off the area where we kneel, inform us that we are trespassing and that we should leave immediately or face arrest.

"Are you going to leave?" the officer asks. I look up and shake my head. No. As we pray "Let peace fill our hearts, our world, our universe," each of us is grabbed by a police officer and placed under arrest. The charge: Failure to quit. You better believe it. Members of the Washington-based Community for Creative Nonviolence and Jonah House, organizers of the daily pray-ins, gathered by the White House fence on Pennsylvania Avenue, clapping and cheering for us as we are led down a driveway and out of public view. They have been coming to the White House every morning for a month; we are the twentieth group they've supported with applause, briefings, answers to legal questions, and prayer.

"Stand facing the wall and put your hands above your head," the police officer orders. One by one we are frisked—very, very thoroughly—and handcuffed, hands behind our back. Then a barrage of identification questions, a Polaroid snapshot with our arresting officer, and into the paddy wagon.

Before the door slams shut, an officer wants to know if we are nuns. "I could tell by the way you prayed," he said. He then takes a few minutes to talk about his spiritual life and how his recent encounter with Christ has thrown his whole life into confusion by forcing him to question his job and his values. "Let us pray for one another," one of the sisters says softly. He nods and with some reluctance locks the door.

When I was arrested in Washington a decade earlier protesting the Vietnam War, I was not prepared for the paddy-wagon ride. So I warn the others to expect a nauseating urine and vomit stench, unbearable heat and no oxygen. Nothing like a pleasant surprise—a clean paddy wagon and a short ride to the district jail.

We are placed in a large holding cell that contains a toilet, a steel picnic table with bench, and a steel shelf without a mattress. Our handcuffs are removed, and we spend the next three hours reading prison graffiti, trying to rest, and praying. Out of sheer exhaustion and anxiety, we play a giddy game of Bible charades. Finally, we are told that our arraignment is tomorrow. We will spend the night in a DC jail.

We are herded back into the paddy wagon and taken to another jail for fingerprints and mug shots. This time the ride is almost unbearable: little oxygen, no fan. It is a muggy day, and we drive for about twenty minutes. Once we park, the officer is kind enough to open the back doors so we can get fresh air, although he makes it clear to us that he is being generous—the doors should stay shut. Thank God for a little compassion because we are kept in the paddy wagon for nearly two hours.

While rolling my fingertips in black muck, the officer tells me I should protest the Congress, not the White House. "They're the ones who voted on the budget," he says. And he's angry. "All those representatives from the poor districts in the South votin' on the budget, robbin' their own people."

We brace ourselves for the ride back but aren't prepared for rush hour and countless traffic delays. Nor for our driver playing the good Samaritan, stopping twice to help motorists. Any other time we'd applaud, but now Marlene is pounding on the thick window asking the officers to please turn on the small ceiling fan so we can breathe. "We can't" the driver shouts back. "One of your demonstrators broke it about two weeks ago."

None of us knows what to expect in the DC jail, and all of us are scared. We try as best we can to strengthen one another as we are led into the jail.

Hundreds of black males rush to the cell doors, climb the bars, hooting and screaming obscenities and pointing to the strange sight—five middle-class white women coming to jail.

Through the windows that separate the prison entrance from the cells, I stare back, long and hard. Never do I want to forget what human beings are capable of: twenty grown men in a cell, arms and legs wrapped around bars, the violent and lustful looks, the inhuman din of a human zoo. The poet claims one can find infinity in a grain of sand. Perhaps, by slowly engraving this scene in my bones, I might find, over the years, a compassionate heart.

A buzzer sounds, a steel door opens, and the officer motions for us to walk through. In a mocking tone he says, "Have a good night, ladies." The door clangs shut, sealing us in the women's section of the DC jail. We find ourselves in a holding cell with a steel shelf to sit on and an open toilet. All of us decide to go to the bathroom while we're among friends. It is the little things like open toilets that we can't be nonchalant about. Hard as we try to take it in stride, our backgrounds, our training, clash violently with this lack of privacy. And we are embarrassed about being embarrassed. None of us wants to admit that we mind going to the toilet in front of strangers.

It seems such a trivial thing, so incongruent with a "heroic" stand against the arms race. I mean, it is so bourgeois, so "nunish"—but, oh, so real. On the other hand, maybe we should be upset. Why isn't there at least a four-foot wall for some privacy? This is yet another instance of the system going out of its way to strip inmates of human dignity.

One by one we are taken from the holding cell, asked some basic ID questions, and then led to our cells. Pat and I share a cell, but Carolyn is alone in hers and there's another empty cot. "I'll probably be getting a roommate," she whispers from the adjoining cell, "so try to stay awake to see if I'm okay." Close to midnight I hear someone calling my name. "Mary Lou," Carolyn whispers, "I heard the guards say the police are bringing in four prostitutes. Stay awake and see what happens to me." I promise to stay alert and in a few minutes hear a woman being locked in her cell. I can't hear their conversation clearly, but it sounds neighborly enough and I drift into a twilight sleep.

"Get up, it's time for breakfast," the guard announces at 4:30 a.m. We are let out of our cell to drink coffee, and soon Marlene and Deni join us. Both of them had spent the night in individual cells.

The morning guard is much friendlier than the lady on night duty. "What do you think of this place," she asks me.

"Not much," I answer, elaborating on the lousy food, the noise, and the lights.

"I never thought about prisons at all until I came to work here," she says. "They're horrible places, horrible. Maybe if more people like you and your friends go to jail and see what they're like, you can help change them."

"Yeah," I answer halfheartedly, not too enamored of the prospect of spending more time in jail.

Carolyn begins telling me about her roommate, Diane, who was picked up for "pushing." "She's taking the rap for her husband because he has a record and can't afford another arrest," Carolyn explains. "We talked for about two hours. It was weird.

Right in the middle of her stories about drugs and a bloody account of a shootout between blacks and a white cop, she started to tell me how her car was filled with plants—not pot, but plants. I told her that I liked plants, too, and here we were at 1 a.m. in the DC jail discussing spider plants and geraniums. I really liked her."

The overnight lockup has room for eight and, besides the five of us and Diane, there are two young women from Nigeria. After coffee, the eight of us are taken back to the holding cell where we join two prostitutes who had spent the night sleeping on a steel shelf and the concrete floor. I feel a pang of guilt. If we hadn't been arrested, those two would have had the minimal comfort of a cot and thin gym mat. God knows, they need a good night's rest more than I do. All of us sit and wait for another hour.

It is a short paddy-wagon ride to the courthouse, where we are taken to the basement, frisked, and locked in a larger holding cell that has two steel shelves and a toilet. Marjorie, a young woman picked up for prostitution, makes a pillow out of the toilet paper roll and stretches out to sleep. When she gets called to the door to answer some questions, Diane crosses the cell and boldly takes her "pillow" and shelf space. I brace for a fight and, sure enough, Marjorie issues the challenge by telling Diane to move her ass. Diane obliges without much of a protest, but Marjorie makes the mistake of ripping off the piece of toilet paper that touched Diane's face. "My black skin bother you, honey?" Diane charges. "One thing I can't stand is an uppity nigger who ain't black like a real nigger. Fancy lady, I bet you sell your pussy on the street corner."

"Yeah, I do," Marjorie brags. "You jealous or somethin'?"

"No, honey, I don't have to sell mine. I got me a husband," Diane slashes back.

The words get more brutal, and I expect to see fists flying soon. But Marjorie refuses to be intimidated and Diane, who looks much tougher and streetwise, backs off.

The tension in the cell has just drifted through the bars when the guards bring in about twenty women who will be sentenced today. The whole crew stops at our cell and stares. "Well, what have we here? Tijuana, come and see what we have here," one of them bitterly cries out.

"Some mother fuckin' white bitches, looks like to me," answers Tijuana. "I bet you're in here for demonstratin', right? What the mother fuck do you really care about the budget? It's not gonna touch your ass. Your fuckin' middle-class families can get you white bitches outta here anytime, right?"

On it goes for about five minutes. I'm so relieved when they're put in a different cell. Deni turns and whispers: "I'm glad I didn't come here to save anyone but myself. It could be devastating." I nod.

One of the women is nine months' pregnant and is put in a separate cell, given a more comfortable chair, and covered with a blanket. Suddenly she jumps up and starts to stuff the blanket through the bars yelling, "Lice, lice." The guard runs in swearing about the laundry service and complaining because the pregnant woman is here in the first place. "We ain't got no provisions down here if sumpin' happens," she mutters. About two hours later the woman is taken to court and one of the guards soon reports that she has gone into labor in the courtroom.

We wait and we wait, the morning only interrupted by legal aides who come to ask more questions and by a lady from the drug and alcohol abuse department who wants a urine sample. The five of us refuse.

I never expected the waiting to bother me like this. It shocked me that I couldn't be at ease with the present moment. It was as if the gray prison walls had begun to seep through my pores and settle inside of me. All my words and actions for peace seemed futile, senseless, and empty. I couldn't pray or concentrate, but struggled merely to maintain an exterior calm. People accuse protestors of being impatient, of expecting change too quickly. Based on this brief experience, I would argue to the death that no one understands waiting more profoundly than those who have been in prison. Into the fifth hour of sitting, Deni asks me, "Do you remember that line from Siddhartha? 'What have you learned that you can give?'

And the answer, 'I can fast, I can think, I can wait.' I think I'm beginning to understand what it means to wait."

We are finally taken upstairs to meet with our lawyer, a student from Georgetown, who, along with others, is doing all the pray-in legal work for free.

The five of us agree to plead guilty and decide not to make individual statements to the judge regarding the arms race. We tell the lawyer to make a statement for us, but to keep it very, very short. None of us has the heart to make one person in prison wait one minute longer than necessary while we give grandiose statements about the immorality of nuclear weapons and our sensitive consciences. Some of these people have been waiting for arraignment or sentencing for months. All we want is to push them out the front door as quickly as possible.

Marjorie asks our lawyer which judge is on the bench. When he answers "Norman," she throws up her hands and shouts, "Alleluia, I'll be working tonight." She tells me, "He's the kindest one we got." The judge she had on Monday hit her with a $250 fine. "I just can't afford another fine like that. I got a kid to feed."

While Marjorie and I are talking, someone starts to cry. Carolyn has her arms around a beautiful young black girl who's tearfully telling her story. When she was only twelve, Malita saw her stepfather shoot her mother. One foster home after another, a series of runaways, and finally reform school followed. Her latest arrest was for possession of drugs, although she claimed to be taking the rap for her boyfriend. Malita has just turned eighteen, and this is her first time in court as an adult. "Sometimes I wish I could wake up and all of this would be a bad dream. There's been nobody since my mother died."

Carolyn hugs her and gives her the Pax address. "You let me know what happens to you," she says. "I'll be sure to write," Malita promises.

I watch the scene and think of a letter I received from Steve Clemens, who is in jail for resistance actions. He wrote: "It may help monasteries to be better in touch with justice questions

regarding prisons if they had some members on the inside—
and what opportunities for mission and service inside."

All those who will be arraigned or sentenced—men and
women—are taken to cells outside the courtroom area. Our
lawyer visits briefly and tells us that the four protesters from
Washington who were also arrested yesterday want to plead
nolo contendere instead of guilty or not guilty. The lawyer
explains that nolo contendere (no contest) means you do not
consider yourself guilty of a crime but feel the government
has enough evidence to prove its case. That is fine with us.

About three o'clock in the afternoon, more than ten hours
after we've been awakened, we are called before Judge Norman.
The government asks that we be given six months' probation
and, during that time, be forbidden to return to the White
House. Norman does his best to have one of us plead not guilty
instead of no contest. It's obvious that he is in sympathy with
our cause and would like one of us to test the government's
charges in court.

But at this moment I don't give a damn about nuclear bombs,
radical Christianity, or nonviolent protest. It's all I can do to
stop myself from screaming, "Please hurry up. Get this over
with, Judge. There are people behind us who have been waiting in miserable conditions for months. You don't know what
it's like. . . . "

The judge accepts our plea of nolo contendere—despite
the government's objections—and sentences us to "time spent."
We are free, but not like yesterday morning. Part of each of us
is still locked up in the DC jail; part of each of us still sits and
waits. It is the least we can do for those we left behind.

Death

I took an afternoon off and felt guilty about my dad. He's
ninety, and I left him home alone for a few hours. He feels bad
that my nights and days revolve around him. I moved back
to my childhood home about four years ago when it became

apparent that he was dying of loneliness, was losing his sight from glaucoma, was not eating well, and was a little afraid to be alone at night. Imagine, my dad, the strongest guy on the east side during his youth, afraid to be alone at night. Then we discovered the cancer that was raging, too.

He sits in his blue recliner trying to watch golf, although the glaucoma makes it increasingly difficult for him to spot the ball. Mostly he sleeps, wrapped in a maroon polartec throw that he got for Christmas. My father is slowly slipping away. I'll be back by early evening, but I feel disloyal leaving him alone even for those few hours.

My father is dying. He took a turn for the worse this week, falling twice and going into sugar shock. I had to call an ambulance. He can hardly walk, hanging on to the walker for dear life. He has caught a cold and is coughing heavily. The doctor tells me that his prostate cancer is raging wildly and the count is up to 275. The doctor says, "I'm afraid, Sister, that we are coming to the end." I am frightened, especially at night, because I don't know what to do if something happens.

My dad went to the hospital because his leg was swelling, and the doctor feared a blood clot. Instead, they found that cancer had spread all through his abdomen. The prognosis is "three months or less." He has a lesion on his heel that makes it impossible for him to walk without a brace. And even with the brace, he shuffles painfully with his walker. When he has to go to the bathroom, it takes too long to put the brace on and he urinates in his pants. Yesterday he urinated in his bed. He sleeps most of the day. I have a wonderful hospice team, Lynn and Collette, and an extraordinary friend, Eileen, who comes twice a day to check on him. Tim, an old friend, came in from Pittsburgh to stay until the end. His presence, and my cousin Jim's, allows me to leave the house a few hours a day. Tim is also very strong and can help lift my father. And I have my friends who eat supper here every night. Rosanne and Mary even take turns staying with me at night. I surprise myself with my nursing skills.

I listen to the prognosis: His legs will continue to swell until he is unable to walk. His penis and scrotum will swell. The water will have nowhere to go, and his legs will start to "weep." He can barely walk now. He stays twenty-four hours a day in his electrically controlled recliner. He wears diapers. He has urine and bowel accidents. I change and wipe him. The indignity of it all is hard on him.

Marty, the deacon from Holy Trinity Church, visited on Holy Thursday and brought a speaker phone. Tonight, when the parish sings "Gorzkie Zale," the traditional Polish Lenten lamentations, the music will be piped into my dad's house. What a beautiful gesture.

Easter morning my dad awakened and told me he felt "like a new man." Twelve people came for breakfast. My father sang the traditional Easter morning hymn and blessed the house. In the afternoon, when Therese and Paul, Florence and Carolyn came for a visit, he sang "Gorzkie Zale" to them. They said it made their Easter.

My dad is now bedridden. We moved a hospital bed to the parlor, right in front of the large bay window. The hardest thing for me is when he says, "I'm getting better." We get a wheelchair, and my brother Joe builds a small ramp so that he can sit outside, one of his favorite activities.

My father decided to die last night. As I was preparing to go to bed, he called: "Mary Lou, I've made my peace with God. I'm ready. But I don't feel God. All my life I felt a presence, like a cloud. But I don't feel that anymore."

"Oh, dad, I love you," I said. "You go to God. You are very close to God. You have brought many people to God. You are the best father a girl could ever have, and I love you. I don't want you to suffer. You go to be with mother. She is waiting."

"Honey, I can't see anymore. I can't hear anymore. I can't get out of bed. And I know I'm not going to get better. I've been so lucky with my children. I can't express how I feel about you and the boys. I don't know how to do it."

"Do you want me to call the boys to come?"

"No, that is not necessary. Please give them my blessing and tell them I am so proud of them."

In the middle of the night he had to urinate.

"How are you," I asked.

"I can't sleep," he said.

"Are you anxious? Do you want a pill?"

"No," he answered. "I am anticipating."

I went to bed and cried for two hours. In the morning I crept to his bedside to see if he had, indeed, died.

"I'm still here," he said, eyes closed. "My heart is too strong."

The next day I told him to tell my brothers how proud he was of them himself. He called each of his sons and said, "I'm going now; I tried to be a good father." It was very poignant.

On Wednesday, he looked to be near death, and people came to hold vigil. So many people came: Mary, Rosanne, Carolyn, Di, Margo, Jim, Mary Jane, Pewee and his girl, Therese, Paul, Tim, Maureen. He seemed to go into a coma around 6 p.m. Then he called to me: "Mary Lou, what am I going to wear in the casket? What did you put in the obit? Who is saying the Mass? Make sure the right songs are sung at the Mass—maybe John can do "Sedeczna Matka" and you and your brothers do "Witaj Krolowa Nieba." Who is bringing Aunt Florence?" We stayed up most of the night.

On Friday he told me that he had enough of talk about death; he wanted to live some more. He wanted to go for a ride. My brother and Tim picked him up and took him for an ice-cream cone and to see my brother Joe's old house. When he got home he was so tired that he passed out and stayed unconscious for twenty-four hours. No one could believe that after his condition on Wednesday night he was in a car on Friday. My brother thinks he wanted to say goodbye to the city.

He had a Polish sausage sandwich today and listened to the golf tournament before falling into a deep sleep.

He was asleep most of the day and then began to get agitated. He started talking aloud and seeing people who were not in the room, at least not present to us. I was up most of the night because he kept calling out and telling me to put on the light to see who was there.

Right before noon he became very agitated, and I gave him an anxiety pill. He wanted pepperoni, and I gave him two small pieces on two crackers. He had a hard time chewing and swallowing. He said he had pain in the groin area, and I gave him half a pain pill. He had a very peaceful night. No reaching with his arms, no calling out.

This morning he said he wanted a final request. When I asked him what, he said a song. When I asked him which one, he said the one his father sang to the family every Easter morning at 6 a.m.—"Wesoly nam dzis dzien nastal" (Rejoice, this is the day Jesus has risen). He then sang the first verse—whispered it, really. I joined him. Then he closed his eyes and fell asleep.

When the end came, it was peaceful. He didn't seem to suffer much. We only had to administer morphine in small doses for the last three days. Compared to what it might have been, it was a blessed death. My brother Joe and I were holding his hand at the end while church bells were ringing, and Mary, Rosanne, and Carolyn were gathered around the bedside. After he became bedridden the house was always filled with friends and family. His sons had spent good time with him. Most of his grandchildren had been able to fly in and say goodbye. All of his nieces and nephews visited or called.

His favorite saying in life was, "I am blessed." He was to the end.

Desert Mother

I first saw the name Amma Syncletica in the book *Desert Wisdom* by Yushi Nomura. As a younger seeker, I was seized by the tales of the desert fathers and eager to sit at their feet. What a surprise to find a woman's name among all those abbas. My consciousness of the women's issue was just kindling, but I remember feeling great joy. A desert mother! In the mid-nineties I was asked to do a book review of *The Life of Blessed Syncletica* by Pseudo-Athanasius. By the time I finished the book, I knew that I had met a good and strong woman, one whom I would have trusted as a spiritual teacher. Why would I trust her with my darkest fears, my most embarrassing thoughts, my deepest secrets?

Concern for the poor is my litmus test for a spiritual teacher, and Syncletica had a great consciousness of the poor. She preached and practiced almsgiving, giving away all her possessions to the poor. The first teaching she shared with the women who gathered around her was, "Do no violence to poor persons, for they are needy."

Next, I was awed by her self-knowledge, evident in the discerning spirit that is so critical to a guide of souls. With great depth and clarity she pointed out the pleasures and pitfalls on the spiritual path; for example, when sadness is helpful and when it turns destructive, the differing temptations in youth and middle age, how easily asceticism can turn to pride, how to spot false humility, the place of anger in spiritual growth, and the battling of demons.

Third, she had great leadership gifts, proof that God's spiritual giants come in both genders. The great Sufi poet and mystic Rumi was struck to the ground upon meeting his spiritual elder, Sham, which translates as "the sun," so brilliant and dazzling was his inner light. Her biographer, Pseudo-Athanasius, pays Syncletica the same compliment. He compares her to the sun, claiming that "those who try to mirror the radiance of her life fall victim to confusion of mind, dazzled, overcome, unstrung by the magnitude of her achievements." Obviously, she was "the sun" for many women, firing them with a burning desire for God. Her description and critique of the plight of women in her society are remarkable for a fourth-century anchorite. No wonder women flocked to her. And there is no doubt about where she would stand on today's feminist agenda.

I am both amazed and grateful that Pseudo-Athanasius preserved the teachings of a woman. He must have been an unusual man. But I wish that Syncletica herself or one of her young women followers had edited the texts. Let us hope that in monasteries around the globe women are writing and promulgating the insights of the ammas who now live among us. If we do not do it for our own, it will not be done. Here is to Societies of Syncletica springing up across the land. Wherever women gather, may they raise a toast to you, Amma.

Dorothy Day

While the morning Angelus bells rang, Carolyn knocked on my door and told me that Dorothy Day was dead. "It was on the 11 o'clock news last night," she said. Normally I go downstairs for meditation, but I pulled the covers tighter and spent the half-hour in bed, letting the news seep through me and settle. Dorothy Day was dead.

My first reaction was relief. She had been bedridden recently and was getting weaker. One hated to see this grand old lady slowly deteriorate. A feeling of emptiness followed. One of the twelve just persons who hold up the world had disappeared. Would we find another?

Lately the temptation to quit wrapped itself around me like a down coat in a winter storm—just close up shop and move on. Goodbye to the whining poor who come for food and rent money and pampers and medicine. And come again. And come again. And come again. No more letters mailed to the waste cans of Congress. No more dramatic peace demonstrations to eat up thirty seconds on the evening news. As for teaching peace in the classroom, let someone who believes in it continue. I've given my time to peace and justice. It's someone else's turn. When the nuclear holocaust arrives, I'll be in the lagoons fishing. Please don't blame me. I tried.

To attribute the malaise to exhaustion or boredom is less than honest. It is a deeper cancer that eats away and, I think, affects many in the peace movement. Nothing I do is quite enough. It's not enough to feed the hungry, to shelter the homeless, to live simply, to write letters to Congress, to teach peace, to leaflet, to fast and do dozens of other acts of peace. Nothing suffices. Look, we are all going to be blown up and I have to do something to stop it. But no, that's not completely true either. I don't believe anything I do will make much difference, but results shouldn't be my concern. I agree with Dan Berrigan, who answers charges of a savior complex by stating: "Ours is a much more modest goal, to bring a little sanity to the times."

I got up to prepare morning prayer in Dorothy Day's honor. Many times she had written of her deep love for the Divine Office and had recited it daily. I automatically opened the breviary to the Office of the Dead. I began reciting Psalm 146 but could barely finish. Tears blurred the words:

> Happy the one whose help is the
> God of Jacob. . . .
> Who keeps faith forever;
> secures justice for the oppressed
> gives food to the hungry.
> The Lord sets captives free;
> the Lord gives sight to the blind.
> The Lord raises up those
> that were bowed down;
> the Lord loves the just.

Nothing spectacular here. Only the need to keep faith.

Easter

The week before Easter the American Cancer Society held its annual fundraiser, selling tens of thousands of daffodils throughout the city. Everywhere in the building where I work there are waves of yellow. One braggart bouquet struts its stuff in the center of my desk.

I admit that part of me is jaded about celebrating Easter.

I don't understand why children in Iraq are blown apart by our bombs. Why my church won't ordain women and even tries to stop us from talking about it. Why a continent named Africa is dying a slow, torturous death from AIDS. Why we help topple a legitimately elected government in Haiti. Why we wash our hands of Palestinian and Israeli blood. Why my nine-year-old neighbor was sexually abused by her father. Why a friend's mother can't afford her cancer medicine. Why children burn cats. Why we cut down the rainforest.

And why religious leaders, politicians, you and I, do little or nothing to stop the carnage. I will sit in the pew at the Easter vigil in a few days and hear the scriptures celebrate the victory of life over death. And part of me will feel like a stranger in both country and church.

The other part will remember that the symbol of Easter is an empty tomb. And I still need to be emptied of my own truths, ideas, and opinions of the Jesus story according to the gospel of Kownacki.

"Everyone discusses my art and pretends to understand, as if it were necessary to understand, when it is simply necessary to love," Monet said about his art. Can't the same be said of the Easter story? I'm part of that "everyone" who discusses Easter and pretends to understand. Haven't I missed the mystery because my tomb is still crammed with the need for proof that unconditional, nonviolent love works?

Why not just love and see what happens? Forget the arguments, the cynicism, the judgments, and try the one thing necessary for Easter to happen. Try to love. Admit that I am clueless when it comes to understanding human suffering and cruelty and try the one thing necessary for Easter to happen. Try to love even when love makes no sense. Try to love even when love doesn't seem to "work."

Just remember that everyday beauty surprises—red flowers burst between rocks, the fog lifts and a blue heron emerges, a college student signs up for the Peace Corps.

Just remember those daffodils that arrive on my desk in Lent. How I hold them close to my face inhaling every last inch of scent and sun, reveling in yellow until beauty becomes unbearable.

Oh, holy, holy time. Oh, feast of love. Let the water of blessing fill me with the one thing necessary to live Easter, not figure it out. Let love, only love, be enough.

Elifet

He was waiting for us at a tourist stop on the final day of our visit. "My name is Elifet, and I am sick," he told us as we climbed out of the Toyota van.

The twelve of us who were in Haiti for a week-long fact-finding tour were oversaturated with scenes of suffering and faces of misery. But Elifet forced us to look again.

Perhaps it was the gentle eyes and soft-spoken words. Maybe it was the jaundiced skin and distended stomach. For sure, it was the tragic story.

"Papa mouri. Mama mouri" (My father is dead; my mother is dead) is how he began. An orphan at twelve, Elifet now lives with his aunt in the village of Fermathe, a destitute mountaintop settlement an hour's drive from Port-au-Prince. Operated on by a U.S. doctor for a rare liver disease, Elifet's fate now depends on a dwindling tourist trade. Shyly he lifts his tattered tee-shirt to show us the long scar. "The doctor promised he would come back, but he never did," Elifet explained. To stay alive, Elifet needs special medicine every two weeks. Usually he walks to the Baptist mission and buys it at a reduced price. This week the mission did not have the medicine. So Elifet had to find a ride to the nearest town where the medicine is much more expensive. We give Elifet money. He deserves to live another fourteen days.

Enemies No More

During the Persian Gulf War a radio station in my hometown ran a contest between Saddam Hussein and the Benedictine Sisters of Erie for "Bad Guy of the Day": Saddam Hussein because he's a clone of Hitler and our Tomahawk missiles were pointed at him; the Benedictine Sisters because we had spoken out and acted against the war. The contest was a cliffhanger, but the Benedictine Sisters eked out a victory.

Before you chalk it up to small town narrow-mindedness, keep two things in mind. First, major companies consider Erie one of the top cities in the nation for testing new products. Will Little Caesar's pizza sell better with two layers of mozzarella or three? Test it in Erie and you'll have a good read of the tempo of the country. Second, Erie is about 65 percent Catholic.

Am I missing something here? Is the church? Is the Catholic peace movement? Why such passion for patriotism and such disdain and misunderstanding toward those who want to rid the world of war?

Then I watched the half-time extravaganza at the Super Bowl during that war and got a clue. Promoters flew in hundreds of children of service men and women to parade around the football field holding flags; a beautiful blond-haired boy sang a special song to the soldiers; there was inspiring military music, an all-American Mickey Mouse, flags and fireworks galore. When the final note sounded, you couldn't find a dry eye in the stadium or in TV rooms across the country. Even my heart was pounding. Someone did an excellent job of marketing patriotism, of making millions feel pride in their country and support for the war. Someone knew that to move the masses you must touch the heart.

Someone, in other words, knows more than the church or the peace movement. So far our approach to war is an appeal to reason or to radical faith—as if getting enough Catholics to memorize and apply the just-war theory will set them afire for peace. Or, if enough pacifists shout "love your enemies" loud and long enough, the crowds will convert.

To be taken seriously in the debate by the military, political, and academic communities, the church and the peace movement seem to be sacrificing legitimate appeals to the heart: symbols and stories that put a human face on war. Points and counterpoints on whether or not a war is just will never affect people's hearts like yellow ribbons on trees and flags on car hoods. Dissecting fine points on what constitutes indiscriminate bombing is meaningless rhetoric to a five-year-old Iraqi girl blown apart by a U.S. cluster bomb. It is that child's story we must tell.

I know what convinced me to dedicate my life to peace. It wasn't attending a seminar on Catholic social teaching. It was reading the novel *All Quiet on the Western Front* by Erich Maria Remarque. The author made me care deeply for Paul, a young German soldier in World War I, a so-called enemy of my country. What an awakening! The "enemy" had a family, best friends, favorite books, loved reading, wrote poems . . . the "enemy" was just like me. I sobbed when Paul went home for a brief furlough; the scene was too close to when my own brother came home from Vietnam, right down to both mothers going to the stove to fry potato pancakes for their war-weary sons.

The Pentagon knows what turned the average U.S. citizen against Vietnam. It wasn't the release of the Pentagon papers, necessary as that was. No, it was watching the news every night and seeing endless rows of body bags holding eighteen-year-old boys from Tacoma and Tempe and Cleveland; it was the newspaper photo of a young Vietnamese girl running down a highway, naked and screaming, her back afire with napalm; it was footage of the dusty village of My Lai strewn with bloody bodies of old women and young children.

When I taught junior-high school, I know what made my students passionate about peace. It wasn't discussing the commandment "Thou Shalt Not Kill." It was literature class, when I had them lie on their backs on the classroom floor and imagine being buried six feet underground while they reverently recited:

> We are the dead.
> Short days ago we lived,
> felt dawn, saw sunsets glow,
> loved and were loved,
> and now we lie in Flanders fields.
>   (John McCrae, 1915)

Another poet, Wilfred Owen, who was himself killed in World War I, wrote: "My subject is war and the pity of war. The poetry is in the pity." The military-industrial complex has as its subject war and the patriotism of war. So far it has done an excellent job of making the U.S. public feel the honor and glory of war.

It is the calling of the peace movement to make people feel the suffering and horror, "the pity of war." It is our calling to put a human face on the "enemy," to help all of us hear the one human heart.

Artists, storytellers, poets, and songwriters can help us. So can ordinary people like the Coast Guard lieutenant who was a crewman on the *Nicholas*, the Navy guided-missile frigate that captured the first twenty-three Iraqi prisoners of war. "I had an image of fierce, ruthless fighters, but, really, these men

weren't different from you or me," he was quoted as saying in
the *Washington Post*. "When I started working with the first
prisoner, I saw the fear in his eyes and saw him shaking. I
think I would have had the same fear if I were in his situation." He continued, "Here's the enemy, but for me, at that
time, it wasn't. It was a life."

Oh, that we would all grasp that insight and stop wasting
time. A radio station that votes for bad guys during a human
tragedy is wasting its time. A church that doesn't connect the
preciousness of life in the womb with the mutilated bodies of
Iraqi babies is wasting its time. A peace movement that relies
on rhetoric rather than making present the human face of war
is wasting its time. And how much more time can we afford to
waste?

Flags

I sent a note to the prioress today requesting that the flag be removed from in front of the monastery. I listed these reasons:

- We are a church that teaches love for all God's people, the whole human family. The national flag of any country is often associated with war and the intent to kill and destroy enemies, God's children.
- Some say the flag is a symbol of freedom, liberty, justice. But for many around the globe—mainly the poor of the earth— the flag means exploitation, military power, and profit at any cost. As women religious we should be on the side of the poor.
- Many religious, academic, and government leaders are telling us that the day of the nation-state is over, that we must begin thinking on an international level if the planet is to survive. Again, we should be prophet to that vision.
- If people see the flag waving in front of the "house of God" or see it next to the tabernacle on the altar, they begin to mix or fuse symbols, identifying God with the flag, religion with the nation. In times of war, many equate their country's actions with God's will or desire.
- Monastic men and women are marginal people who live on the fringe of society. They owe their allegiance only to God. The monastery building itself, all its décor and

environment, should reflect that radical commitment to the "other."

Food

I like this story about food:

Because the tea shop was crowded, a man took the other chair at a table occupied by a woman and ordered tea. As it happened, he was a Jamaican black, though that is not essential to the story. The woman was prepared for a leisurely time, so she began to read the paper. As she did so, she took a cookie from the package. As she read, she noticed that the man across also took a cookie from the package. This upset her greatly, but she ignored it and kept reading. After a while, she took another cookie. And so did he. This unnerved her and she glared at the man. While she glared, he reached for the fifth and last cookie, smiled and offered her half of it. She was indignant. She paid her money and left in a great hurry, enraged at such a presumptuous man. She hurried to her bus stop and opened her purse to get her fare. And then she saw, much to her distress, that in her purse was her package of cookies, unopened.

Here are some thoughts this story provoked in me: Why did the woman presume the food was hers? Do I believe that the extra food in my cupboard belongs to me? Does the United States believe it owns the food that the poor people of the world desperately need? Do soup kitchens, food pantries, and food banks across the country believe they own what is donated to their care?

Our attitude toward food is easy to track. Do we hoard food? Do we make the poor grovel and beg for food? Do we portion food to the poor like misers doling out precious coins? Do we rant and rave that the poor are ripping off the system when someone lies and gets two bags of food at a pantry instead of one? Do we divide the poor into "deserving" and "undeserving" and treat the latter with less kindness? Do we expect the poor to thank us when we give them our extras or leftovers or even when we give of our sustenance? Do we measure poor people's desire for good times and celebrating by different criteria than our own? If we answer yes to any of these questions, we are as mistaken as the woman in the story. Food does not belong to us.

On the other hand, if we bake bread and pass it out for free, if we prepare a feast and throw open the doors to the poor, if food flows in great abundance from our storehouses to the streets where the hungry stand, if we fill empty plates to overflowing and insist that all return for another helping . . . and another . . . and still another . . . then we resemble the gentleman in the story. He understood that food is not for possessing, it is for sharing. After all, whose food is it anyway?

Forgiveness

When they found the body of five-year-old Lila in a dumpster, my friend Sister Mary Miller told me, "I'm afraid if I met the murderer, I'd want to tear his heart out." She probably voiced the sentiments of most of the city of Erie, Pennsylvania. For fourteen days the entire city had searched for Lila. She had occupied the front page of the Erie newspapers. All places of business, buses, and telephone poles were blanketed with posters of her innocent, smiling face. Churches and synagogues had offered special prayers for her safety.

The morning after the child's badly decomposed body was discovered, the phone rang at our priory. Mary, who is director of our soup kitchen and food pantry, was called to the phone. "Sister Mary, it's me, George. I've got to see you right away."

"The minute I heard his voice I knew it concerned Lila," Sister Mary said. George and his three boys lived across the street from Lila's family. They were two poor families eking out an existence in a tough neighborhood. Minutes after the phone call, Sister Mary was in George's home, trying to be present to a father who had volunteered at Emmaus pantry and whose son was charged with the unimaginable crime. George asked Sister Mary to accompany him to jail that afternoon, "to give my son some spiritual help."

Less than twenty-four hours after she had threatened to rip his heart out, Sister Mary sat facing seventeen-year-old Scott. The accused murderer was not a faceless stranger but a boy she knew—a teenager who had accompanied his father to the pantry a few times. "I needed as much spiritual help as he did," Sister Mary confided. "My heart was full of anger and rage."

According to Mary, her meeting with Scott went something like this: "This is very difficult for me, Scott," she said. "I don't know what to say to you. If this charge is true, then what you've done is a terrible thing, an act most people find unforgivable. All I can do is to tell you about the God I believe in, the God I pray to. That God, Scott, has promised to forgive the most terrible crimes, provided we are sorry. If you killed little Lila, her family may never forgive you, and maybe they shouldn't. Your family, friends, and neighbors might not forgive you either. God, however, is a different story. I don't know if you pray, Scott, but if you did this, then sometime today get down on your knees and beg forgiveness. If you are truly sorry, God will forgive you. Please remember that. Do you understand?" The boy merely nodded and stared vacantly ahead.

"I don't believe cheap forgiveness is a solution," Sister Mary said to me later. "Anger in this case is a justifiable emotion and people like Lila's family and myself have to work through it. If we lie about the anger and mouth words of easy forgiveness, it only means we will act out the pain in other ways. Anyway, it was the best I could do. I certainly believe in a God of unlimited forgiveness and compassion, but it was a stark reminder of how far I am from the scripture—'Be compassionate as your God is compassionate.'"

G

Gandhi

After seeing the movie *Gandhi*, I've been thinking about his "experiment with truth."

Thought one: to commit civil disobedience or not. Two years ago I read an interview with Jack Nelson that raised some disturbing questions for me. Nelson, while acknowledging the need for civil disobedience and going to jail, added this qualifier: "I feel that in some instances, people are choosing the option of jail from a place of hardness of heart rather than a place of compassion. . . . They find it easier to survive in that atmosphere than they do in talking to their neighbors and in dealing with the discrepancy between where their neighbors are and the urgency they themselves feel."

His words rang true for me. It's easier and more glamorous for me to get arrested at the White House protesting war than to hold a meeting in my Aunt Louise's living room on the Soviet threat.

While the acceptance of suffering can be a proof of love, it can also demonstrate hardness of heart. Gandhi called it *duryagraha*, stubbornness, rather than *satyagraha*, truth force. Giving your all doesn't necessarily mean you're right. Witness the legions who plowed through hell for Hitler, the thousands who sacrificed themselves for Khomeini, the hundreds who died for Jim Jones. Always keep the words of Paul engraved in the heart, "If I give away all I have, and if I deliver my body to be burned, but have not love, I gain nothing" (1 Cor 13:3).

Thought two: How does a satyagrahi treat the opponent? Gandhi
said that a nonviolent experimenter with truth is never afraid
to trust the opponent. He wrote, "Even if the opponent plays
him false twenty times, the *satyagrahi* is ready to trust him the
twenty-first time, for an implicit trust in human nature is the
very essence of his creed."

I remember an interaction that took place between a group
of demonstrators sitting on the Pentagon lawn and a motor-
cycle cop who pulled up to talk with them. One of the group
said to him testily, "If you want to join us, we'll give you ten
seconds to take off your uniform." Another sharply asked him
to leave. The group members then gathered up their things
and took off across a parking lot, explaining, "We don't talk in
front of cops."

This distrust, even disdain, for the supposed opponent
seemed present at a trial I attended for some resisters. I left
the courtroom feeling great empathy for the judge, who appeared to be struggling with personal sympathy for the defend-
ants' conscience and the demands of the law. When the judge
said, "I am agonizing over this case; it is the most difficult of
my career," I believed him.

Yet, to read an account of the proceedings in a movement
newsletter made me wonder if I had been in the same courtroom—so negative, so smug, so self-righteous was its inter-
pretation of the judge's motives, words, and actions. He was
not treated as a person but as an enemy. If this is an "experiment with truth," I am a stranger in my own home.

In contrast to these individuals was John Leary, a friend
who died unexpectedly at a very young age. Often John would
go by himself to Draper Laboratories, a Cambridge nuclear-
weapons research facility, to distribute holy cards to employ-
ees, to "opponents." One Christmas leaflet written by John
consisted of the familiar peace prayer of Saint Francis of Assisi
and a brief commentary concluding with this appeal:

We share this prayer with you in memory of Christ, the
Prince of Peace. It has special meaning for us and we hope

for you as well. Whatever disagreements we may have concerning the right path to peace, we know that it is a value and a dream you share with us. We hope this prayer will deepen our personal commitment to peace and help open ways for us to work together to eliminate all war, injustice and fear.

I think this is the spirit of reconciliation that Gandhi preached and lived.

Thought three: on symbolic actions. During the movie *Gandhi* I flinched and squirmed when he gave his first speech to the Indian National Congress Party. "I know that what we say here means nothing to the masses," Gandhi told the movement heavies. "Here we make speeches for each other and those liberal English magazines that might grant us a few lines, but the people of India are untouched; their politics are confined to bread and salt." Substitute the words *perform symbolic actions* for "make speeches" and *radical peace magazines* for "liberal English magazines" and you have a picture of the U.S. peace movement.

Gandhi found a way to reach those masses whose politics were "confined to bread and salt." When Gandhi launched his salt march, asking the Indian people to make their own salt rather than purchase English salt, every illiterate and poor person in India understood the action and could participate. We have yet to find an action that unites the masses against oppression and violence, although I must admit that one of my favorites was a fellow in the Midwest who danced on top of a bomb site, crucifix in hand, "exorcising" the evil demons. Hammering on the nose cones of missiles in order to "beat swords into plowshares" is also clear, but it does not touch the lives of ordinary people.

Thought four: on prayer. "The only time our peace community prays is before we commit a protest action," a visitor told our peace group. The only time? That could be an exercise in self-deception, using prayer to convince ourselves that what we do is inspired by God. For Gandhi, prayer was regular and constant, always open to an unexpected truth.

If there is a flaw in the movie about Gandhi, it is that it missed the depth of the spirituality on which his nonviolence rested. Ashram community prayer was so integral to the daily schedule that Gandhi could say with authenticity, "My greatest weapon is mute prayer."

Gestures

A monk's tears, a message in the sand, and a sister with Alzheimer's. In each of these stories I experienced a senseless gesture that pushed open—just a crack—the mausoleum door that closes so much of the human heart to poetry, wonder, and surprise.

The monk's tears belong to Ryokan, the Japanese poet. They tell this story about him. Once a relative of Ryokan's asked the monk to speak to his delinquent son. Ryokan came to visit the family home but did not say a word of admonition to the boy. He stayed the night and prepared to leave the following morning. As the wayward boy was helping tie Ryokan's straw sandals, he felt a warm drop of water on his shoulder. Glancing up, the boy saw Ryokan, eyes full of tears, looking down at him. Ryokan departed silently and the boy soon mended his ways.

The message in the sand belongs to Jesus. In the story the Pharisees brought an adulterous woman to Jesus and demanded that she be stoned to death in accordance with the law. Jesus responded with the words "Let the one among you without sin throw the first stone" and a senseless gesture—he bent down and wrote in the sand. He kept writing until one by one the Pharisees slipped away and Jesus told the woman to "go and sin no more."

In this gesture Jesus was being senselessly kind, and the self-righteous came to self-knowledge. In the gesture he was senselessly hospitable, embracing both accusers and accused, and lives were changed. In the gesture he was senselessly just and confronted a system that oppressed women, challenging us to do the same.

Sister Edna, a retired language teacher, was an Alzheimer's victim who wandered through our monastery emptying people's mailboxes, striking up strange but pleasant conversations, and collecting items from sisters' bedrooms and giving them to others.

One evening one of our high school teachers went to answer a phone call and left her midterm exams and grade book on a table in the community room. When she returned, they were gone. A frantic two-day search followed. There were notes on the bulletin board and pleas on the public-address system. "I need my tests and grade book, Sisters. Report cards are due. Has anyone seen them?"

Finally, someone thought of the wandering collector, Sister Edna, and searched her room. Buried under her towels and other laundry were the grade book and the tests. She had finished grading the tests. Everyone got an A.

"There is no end to the birth of God," D. H. Lawrence wrote. And Edna is indisputable evidence of this insight. Through her seemingly foolish actions we have an in-breaking of the reign of God. Edna, an incarnation of God the Foolish One, wanders the halls reminding us not to fear the final judgment. There are no record books, and everyone is getting an A.

No doubt about it, what appears senseless is often most meaningful. Sometimes we are senselessly tender—like Ryokan, who wept out of love—and hardened hearts begin to melt. Sometimes we are senselessly poetic—like Jesus, who wrote in the sand—and the world is charged with a moment of grace and beauty. Sometimes we are senselessly nonjudgmental—like Sister Edna, who gave everyone an A—and we get a glimpse into the nature of God.

Life is filled to overflowing with these opportunities. All of us have the chance to make the senseless meaningful to the irrationally rational world we live in. If only we would grasp the opportunity. What if we were senselessly vulnerable and reduced the military budget? Might the world know less fear? What if we were senselessly forgiving and rid the country of the death penalty? Would the children understand respect for life? What if we were senselessly generous and revamped the welfare system so the poor had a real chance? Might our own hearts be softened?

   Needless to say, I stay close to experts of the seemingly senseless: the mystics, poets, clowns, and those the rational world labels irrational. And I look for teachers who write in the sand.

Ghosananda

"What a society does to its children, its children will do to society," a Roman sage wrote. What picture comes to your mind when you read that quotation?

   Do you see long lines of hungry children in Africa? Or do you see a child eating a hot meal at a day-care center? Do you see children huddled in bombed buildings in Kosovo? Or do you see children laughing and playing games together? Do you see children sitting alone watching television in empty apartments? Or do you see children being read to by volunteers in after-school programs?

   Certainly the culture of violence seems to dominate. Children are denied education, food, shelter, and medicine in two-thirds of the world. Millions of children are sentenced to early death or robbed of full human life. Even in the United States, the richest country in the world, we are waging a war on children: a violence-saturated media, children shooting children to settle conflicts. And there is the hidden, institutionalized violence that kills both the bodies and spirits of our children. "I never knew we were supposed to eat three times a day," one eight-year-old boy said at the newly opened Kids' Cafe in inner-city Erie.

   The culture of violence can numb. That's why I turn to the example of Venerable Maha Ghosananda, the renowned Buddhist monk who is a beacon of light for the suffering poor of Cambodia. When a writer asked him what he was currently doing, Ghosananda said that he was working to get an international ban against land mines because in Cambodia so many people were getting killed or maimed by them.

When the writer asked how she could help, Ghosananda replied, "You must ask everyone you meet to sign a petition against land mines." Then he reached into the sleeve of his long orange robe, withdrew a petition, and handed it to her. The writer reflected on this simple gesture and concluded, "May we all be not more than one sleeve-length away from connecting our commitment to a peaceful heart to our commitment to a peaceful world."

Good Friday

I was typing a sentence condemning the brutal bombing of Iraqi children when she came into my study, pulled my chair from the desk, took my hand, and cried, "Hurry." We raced two blocks to an abandoned house where a front yard had just been attacked and overtaken by wild violets, by Johnny-jump-ups. We stood in silence for three long minutes and cheered the victory of beauty.

It is because I believe in the victory of beauty that I have walked in the annual Good Friday Pilgrimage for Peace sponsored by the Benedictine Sisters of Erie since 1980. By putting one foot in front of the other for seven miles, one can learn a lot about the journey from evil to beauty, from despair to hope.

The pilgrimage begins in the inner city and winds its way to the monastery outside the city, stopping periodically to pray at stations where the body of Christ suffers today. We stop at the soup kitchen, where we are reminded that in the United States our city holds the dubious distinction of having the highest percentage of minority children living in poverty. There is a tavern that markets nude dancing, a symbol of how society encourages the exploitation and degradation of women.

Except for the prayers at the seven stations, the entire walk is done in silence. Parents with children, the lame in wheelchairs, the elderly, college students, and sisters—about 150 ordinary people—follow a simple wooden cross for the three-hour observance.

Once at the monastery, the pilgrims process into the chapel for the traditional Good Friday service with its readings, prayers, and adoration of the cross. After each pilgrim kisses the huge wooden cross and receives the broken body of Christ, the tabernacle door is closed, the altar is stripped, and silence returns. One could be left in despair, except that from the balcony comes the sound of a bell and two cantors sing over and over: "It is finished in beauty. It is finished in beauty." Then the final bell and the final silence.

Ah, yes, it is finished in beauty.

Tenacious wild violets erupting year after year no matter how many children are tortured worldwide is a glimmer of hope that God's plan for creation will triumph. Ordinary people participating in a seven-mile peace pilgrimage year after year despite growing lines at soup kitchens and escalating violence in our cities is a hope that death will not have the final word.

It is no mistake either, I believe, that Mary Magdalene first looked on the risen Jesus that early morning on the first day of the week, just after sunrise, and saw, of all things, a gardener. Our task is not about death, the empty tomb, and the empty shroud. It is about planting and sowing and caring for hope in whatever garden we find ourselves.

At the Easter Vigil in our monastery chapel, a sister dances the Alleluia banner down the center aisle, accompanied by hand bells and a congregation of hundreds singing "Alleluia."

Two dozen people process down the side aisles carrying flowers of every color and fragrance. In less than a minute an empty sanctuary is transformed into an overpowering garden of lilacs and tulips and hyacinths and daffodils. Hold fast to hope, the fragile flowers shout.

Ah, yes, it is finished in beauty.

Gratitude

Once the Master was at prayer. The disciples came up to him and said, "Teach us how to pray." This is how he taught them:

Two men were walking through a field when they saw an angry bull. Instantly they made for the nearest fence, with the bull in hot pursuit. It soon became evident to them that they were not going to make it, so one man shouted to the other. "We've had it! Nothing can save us. Say a prayer. Quick!"

The other shouted back, "I've never prayed in my life, and I don't have a prayer for this occasion."

"Never mind," his friend yelled. "The bull is catching up with us. Any prayer will do."

"Well, I'll say the one I remember my mother used to say before meals: For what we are about to receive, O God, make us truly grateful."

That story brings a smile . . . and a deep truth. "For what we are about to receive, O God, make us truly grateful" is the only prayer there is. It's a tough one. I figure I've been present for thousands of prayer services in my life so far, but I don't have a clue if I've ever said a prayer, let alone learned the prayer of gratitude.

Despite my desire to pray, I still lack a sense of awe at the gift of the ordinary. I know that nothing I receive is deserved—not the rising sun or the fragrance of a cherry blossom or the smile of a child. Yet rarely do I take time to be grateful. I still complain too much about the gifts overflowing from God's bag of goodness. Instead of rejoicing in a new day, I find fault with the cold and rain. Rather than enjoy the task before me, I desire something more exciting. Instead of accepting life's unexpected but normal turns—unkindness, a broken dream, a loss—I wallow in self-pity. You get the idea.

I also get confused about how to be grateful for truly horrible things I receive. How can I be grateful for the multiplication of nuclear weapons, for more and more hungry children to feed at our soup kitchen, for suicide bombers blowing innocent people to dust, for the taste of 9/11 ashes still on my tongue?

Brother David Steindl-Rast, a Benedictine writer I admire, offers an opinion. He writes that I don't have to be grateful for these things in and of themselves, but I can be grateful for the opportunity to do something about them. He reasons that being centered in the present moment with a grateful heart can inspire a creative response, no matter how humble.

You can see that I'm still a beginner here. "For what I am about to receive, O God, make me truly grateful." I figure that if I really, really become this prayer, then my questions will disappear. I also know that I will only develop a grateful heart by practice. I have to practice being grateful for what I receive by being grateful. That's why I keep going to prayer.

"It is gratefulness which makes the soul great," Abraham Heschel wrote. And so we pray to become great souls. For what we are about to receive, O God, make us truly grateful.

Guilty Bystander

When I was a child, I used to imagine being in Jerusalem on that first Good Friday. I was quite a hero in my youth. No crowd could intimidate me. "Free him," I would have yelled, "the man is innocent." If they persisted in their death march, I would have broken through the mob and helped Jesus carry the cross to Calvary, pleading with the Roman soldiers to take me instead of Jesus. At the very least I would have stood by him to the end, no rooster-crowing Peter's blood flowed through these veins.

But now that I am older, it occurs to me that two thousand years ago I would have done exactly what I do today. Practically nothing. How do I know? Simple. I say I believe the words of Jesus, "What you have done to the least of my brethren, you have done to me." Thousands of people are being tortured to death around the world. Children are hungry everywhere. At least one woman is raped every time my living room clock ticks another sixty seconds. And so on and so on. Do I work to end these horrors? Where is the sense of urgency, the passion? As Merton would say, a guilty bystander.

$\mathcal{H}$

●●●●●●●●●●●●●●●●●●●●●●●●●●●●●●●

Haiti

Haiti is the only third-world country that I have visited. But my four visits there gave me enough meditation material to last a lifetime.

Consider Haiti's brightly colored, hand-painted mini-buses, which are called tap-taps. All of Haiti's poor, 80 percent of the population, 4.6 million people, depend on these buses to haul them from place to place. On each of these tap-taps, which flood the city like circus wagons in the daytime and like moving Christmas light displays at night, the owner paints a name. Imagine my confusion when in the midst of unimaginable poverty, destitution and squalor I saw tap-taps bearing the names *Merciful Jesus, Tranquility,* and *God Is Good.*

How can those enduring such suffering still celebrate? The tap-taps *are* a celebration, a symbol of joyful Haitian hearts, a loud proclamation that people trapped in unbelievable destitution can still participate in the dance of life.

Contrast the song of joy coming from the tap-taps with the faces you see in the country club or in the shopping malls or in your dining room or in the mirror. Does spiritual writer Rabbi Zalman Schacter-Shalomi draw our portrait when he writes: "There is a disease rampant—a chronic low-grade depression that never knows how to smack its lips and say, 'It is good to be alive'"?

Another question: How can those with so little have such grateful hearts? *God Is Good* and *Thank You, Jesus* are tap-tap billboards that dot their muddy roads. How can we who have so much be so ungrateful, so dissatisfied, so greedy for more? Visitors who return from a third-world country are branded forever by the hospitality and generosity pressed upon them by the poor. Stories abound about peasant families giving their last egg or killing their only chicken to treat visitors.

Please don't misunderstand. I don't want to reinforce the conventional wisdom that the poor are happy in their misery, content on the dung heap. I've devoted most of my adult life to exposing that "wisdom" as a lie, to making visible the oppression under which two-thirds of the world's people live. I do not want to temper the cutting edge of the scripture that demands that we let justice roll down like a river.

No, the poor are not happy that their babies die of hunger. They are not happy scavenging through garbage for food. But the poor do have, I believe, a more profound understanding of what it means to be dependent on God. And that, I think, is the source of their joy and generosity.

Because the poor possess nothing, they don't grasp anything. Because the poor have so few material goods, they are grateful for what God gives and share it more easily.

How desperately we need the gifts of the poor. How essential for our spiritual liberation that we pray the scriptures with them, that we struggle side by side with them. How necessary for our salvation that they free us from the possessions that possess us and enable us to taste deep joy once again.

Health Board

This week our soup kitchen received its annual visit from the Health Department. Every visit means purchasing new equipment. Last year we had to put in a new floor. This year they want us to put plexi-glass covering around the peanut butter and the bread in case one of the guys sneezes. Imagine! The people who come to the soup kitchen sleep in the cold, don't have warm clothing, don't get enough to eat, and the

Health Department worries about protecting them from sneezes.

Holy Fools

Jim hadn't spoken a coherent sentence in eight years. A regular at the Emmaus Soup Kitchen in Erie, Jim babbles on for hours in non-stop sentences.

One day a volunteer brought her newborn to the kitchen and was showing him to the guests. When Jim looked at the baby, the confused look disappeared from his eyes and he said in a loud and clear voice: "I was like that once. I'd like to be like that again." The clarity lasted only a few seconds, and then Jim returned to his other world.

In that moment Jim became a holy fool, one of the "mad" prophets who shout truths that lie hidden in each heart. Don't we all groan inwardly for the child to be born anew in our lives?

That's why I try to stay alert to the "mad" among us. I need holy fools like Jim to stir my cynical and jaded heart with a message of new life.

One holy fool is John, an old Russian Orthodox believer who helps serve Christmas dinner at our soup kitchen each year. After washing the dishes, John bid a few stragglers a "blessed Christmas" and prepared to leave. That's when he noticed one of the guests wrapping plastic bags around his torn sneakers. John took off his shoes and gave them to the man. Then he trudged home through the snow in his socks.

My brother Jerry is a "madman." He runs a convenience store in Erie's inner city. "Sis, when the neighborhood kids told me they weren't getting anything for Christmas, I couldn't stand it," he explained. So for three hours on Christmas day he gave away free pop, potato chips, and pretzels to the children—all they could eat and drink. He even ordered cheese and cold-cuts platters for them and opened all the video games for free. The small store was wall-to-wall children.

The third holy fool appeared to a friend of mine in the middle of winter on a freezing night when she and a friend were being driven home from a party. They were stopped for a red light in downtown Erie when a street person, wrapped in a blanket, walked in front of the car. The driver rolled down the window and shouted, "Why don't you get a job so you have a place to live, you bum." Both women simultaneously yelled at the driver to be quiet and reached into their purses for money. My friend handed a bill to the man saying, "Please find a place to stay." The man stopped, opened the blanket he was wearing for a coat, and pulled out a red rose. Yes, a red rose in December. He smiled and handed it to my friend and walked away.

The old Russian, my brother, and the street person leap into the unexpected. Their gestures of love lift for a moment the shroud that covers the new person waiting to be born in each of us. How our sanity and survival depend on these fools; how alert and aware we must be to their presence.

On Saturday, December 2, 1989, the ninth anniversary of the deaths of the four U.S. women who were raped and killed in El Salvador for advocating for the poor, I participated in a protest in Washington, DC. About fifty representatives of church groups were arrested for praying in front of the White House to protest the latest killing and harassment of church leaders in that war-torn country. The arrests took longer than usual, so I spent a good part of the afternoon kneeling and sitting on the cold pavement. Though I joined in the prayer and song of the group, my mind was elsewhere. Mostly I was looking at the faces—there were dear friends here. For over twenty years many in this group have spent long afternoons demonstrating in front of the Pentagon, the South African embassy, the Capitol, and Trident submarine bases.

Perhaps it was the gray December day, but I felt weary and barren of spirit. I ached for the zeal of Jane, who believed her action mattered. I would have welcomed the nervousness of Nathan, who was being arrested for the first time. But mostly I felt like Jim, just babbling meaningless messages and going through routine rituals. No newborn awakened in me.

After being arraigned and released, I spent the evening watching a Peter, Paul, and Mary holiday special on public television. Talk about the faces of dear friends—how many years have these three hammered out justice all over the land? During one song children came on stage and each one lit a candle as Peter, Paul, and Mary, the children's choir, and the audience sang:

> Don't let the light go out,
> It's lasted for so many years.
> Don't let the light go out,
> Let it shine through our love and our tears.

Like mad fools, Peter, Paul, and Mary were pleading that the peace message be passed to the next generation. The children's faces were aglow; the audience was in tears. And me? It was as if someone held a child before me and lifted it on high. I whispered: "I was like that once. I'd like to be like that again."

Hope

I was part of a group of 150 churchwomen who attempted a peace pilgrimage to Honduras in December 1983. Our plan was to pray for peace at U.S. naval and air bases as a witness against the military aid given to Contras in that troubled region. Before departing for Tegucigalpa, we spent an orientation day in Miami, and I had an opportunity to get acquainted with hope, to discover its depths, and to confront my shallowness. Prior to the trip I would have placed myself in the top 5 percent of any test on hope. My personal assessment: faith is adequate, charity needs lots of work, hope is excellent. Then I went to Honduras and found out that I failed the ultimate criterion for hope. I discovered I was afraid to die.

I had approached the journey feeling on par with any martyr. Maybe my first mistake was paging through *Cry of the People* by Penny Lernoux one hour before departing for Miami. The section on Honduras let me know I was going to demonstrate in a country where people who think like I do have been baked alive in bread ovens and had their bodies slowly hacked to pieces.

It didn't help when the sister who picked me up at the airport greeted me with, "Gosh, are you brave. I'd never do what you're doing." Then she detailed the vigilante threats and attacks that were taking place in Miami against those who opposed U.S. military aid to Central America. "We've had to keep this whole meeting a secret," she said. "We're afraid of being shot at again."

I wondered what it meant when the Honduran bishops who had originally pledged their support for the pilgrimage suddenly withdrew it. Was it just their conservative bent, or were they trying to send a warning?

For two nights I tossed and turned in bed, trying to calm myself, putting my fate in God's hands by repeating my favorite prayers. But it was no use. I felt nothing but deep, deep fear. Whether the cause of my fear was real or imaginary or exaggerated does not matter. What counts is that at a new level I recognized the cost of discipleship and recoiled from the cross.

Saint Augustine tells us that hope has two lovely daughters, anger and courage—anger that things are not what they ought to be and courage to make them what they must be. Relief, not anger, was what I felt when the Honduran military boarded our plane on the runway at Tegucigalpa and told us we were not welcome there. I said a prayer of quiet thanksgiving instead of a prayer for renewed courage when the plane flew back to Miami.

In her book *Bringing Forth Hope*, Denise Priestley captures the struggle between hope and hopelessness by using the symbol from Chapter 12 of the book of Revelation: a woman gives birth while a dragon stands before her ready to devour the child. Priestley writes: "The woman had only the promise of God to hold on to as she confronted the dragon and death. . . . She *hopes* by looking the dragon right in the eyes and continuing to give birth."

In the stare down between the dragon and myself, I blinked.

The night of our aborted trip to Honduras, NBC was showing *Choices of the Heart*, a movie based on the life of Jean Donovan, one of four U.S. missionaries who were raped and murdered in El Salvador for their work with the poor. In the final scene Jean Donovan was talking about her friend, Ita Ford, one of the other women who was killed. She was recounting how Ita had almost drowned a few months before. During a storm Ita and another sister drove off a road into a river. Her friend was killed, and Ita told Jean that she felt herself drowning, too, trapped under water.

"I didn't even struggle," she told Jean. "I felt myself going under and said, 'Receive me, Lord, I'm coming.'"

These words fastened themselves to my heart, and I listened to them all night long. I can still hear them. "Receive me, Lord, I'm coming." Amazing. Amazing hope.

7

Important Things

Everybody is into evaluation of at-risk children these days. You have to prove that running a kids' cafe or an after-school art house for at-risk children is worthwhile, that it "changes" the children, or else funding is difficult. Mostly people want us to demonstrate that school grades go up because we feed the children dinner; teach them to examine who they are through art, poetry, and music; and offer a safe, nurturing oasis for a few hours a day.

I am all for change and improvement, but when I look back on my own life I realize that some major childhood influences did not bear fruit until adulthood. For example, a story that I read in seventh grade by Leo Tolstoy about the presence of God in each person didn't hit home until I was in my twenties. I wrote stories in the middle grades, was encouraged by parents and teachers, then didn't pick up a pen until many years later. Based on my experiences and the life stories of almost everyone I know, I think we should fund safe places for children, where caring adults are present—even if school test scores go down. We should take a chance on *maybe*, on *what if?*

If scores do go up, great. But what I think is important can't be measured . . . at least not yet. The sister at the Kids' Cafe keeps a toy tea set in the kitchen. Every day four of the girls ask Sister Sallie for the tiny tea cups and saucers, pour a bit of milk, and—here's the good part—ask one other person to join them for tea. Sometimes it's an adult volunteer, often it's another child. "What do you do at the tea party?" Sister Sallie asked them. "We talk about important things," the little girls told her. That's enough proof for me that the Kids' Cafe is a success: four little girls spending fifteen minutes talking about important things.

Inner-city Neighborhood Art House

No one understands the roots of rage and alienation found in our youth. We are all frightened, appalled, and sent searching for solutions every time there is a school shooting, a gang rape by eleven year olds, wanton acts of cruelty or ordinary theft, defacing of property, drug use by elementary school children.

We cast our net: The vulgarity and callousness of the culture of TV, movies, and music. Easy access to guns. Broken homes. Latchkey kids. Lack of parental care and responsibility. The decline of a common value system. All of these combined with the emotional turmoil of adolescence.

During the week of one of the school shootings in our country, Poetry Alive, a national poetry drama troupe for students, did a workshop at our Inner-City Neighborhood Art House. The Art House offers free lessons in the visual, performing, and literary arts to six hundred at-risk children each year through after-school and summer programs. I'm not claiming that the solution to children's violence is a program like Poetry Alive, but let's look at what these five days contributed.

First, the children learned the skills of public speaking. They had to stand in front of an audience and be loud, clear, and engaging. I learned in a workshop once that a study to determine what similarities, if any, existed among those who had risked their lives to save Jews during the Holocaust revealed this: Most of the heroic had performed publicly as children. They had learned to stand on their own two feet. They achieved a sense of self-accomplishment, self-awareness, and self-confidence. Mahatma Gandhi, the nonviolent liberator of India, started alternative schools in his nonviolent communities.

Every day began with the arts and with a performance of some kind by the children. Gandhi thought this was essential to building self-reliant and courageous individuals—the type of individual who in time of conflict or crisis draws upon inner resources and does not bend to peer pressure. Second, the children at the Art House learned to memorize one or two poems. "You are what you think," the Buddha said. What thoughts do you want running through your child's head? Which words do you think build sensitivity and self-respect? The violent, anti-woman, anti-gay lyrics of the hip-hop scene or this from Langston Hughes:

> Hold fast to dreams
> For if dreams die
> Life is a broken-winged bird
> That cannot fly.

> Hold fast to dreams
> For if dreams go
> Life is a barren field
> Frozen with snow.

Third, the children learned to work together. They were put in groups of four, given a poem, and together had to determine the characters, the setting, the action, and the script. The children disagreed, but, with the pressure of a performance, knew they needed one another. They practiced civility and the give-and-take of social situations. In the end it was a group victory, and it built community.

Nothing earth shattering at first glance. But what if this experience and others like it were repeated day after day? This is the philosophy behind the Inner-City Neighborhood Art House: if we put art and beauty and values into the lives of children, we will reap soul. Would children have a better chance to develop their potential if a few times a week they were exposed to a painting by Monet, Picasso, or O'Keefe instead of the violent and sexually explicit images of MTV and BET? Would their souls be richer if every day they listened to Bach and learned to play Mozart, if they heard the lyrics of Sandburg and Dickinson every day, not just the latest version of Eminem? What if our children developed self-confidence and self-esteem by performing and learning to play an instrument, painting pictures from what is inside themselves, and dancing to Swan Lake? What if they memorized words that were inspiring or humorous rather than violent and nihilistic? What if they learned to work with their peers for a common goal where all shared in the applause? Would this help instill compassion, empathy, and tolerance? Would this dent the culture of violence?

I still remember the day when ten-year-old Johnny, one of our most talented students, left us. A well-known local artist was so impressed with Johnny's work that she was arranging to have private lessons with him. Johnny came to the Art House after school that day, just as he had for four years. Right in the middle of a class his father came in and told him to get his coat and collect his framed art pieces that were hanging on the walls—they were leaving for Florida. "I love it here," he sobbed to Sister Anne, director of the Art House. "Please tell everyone thank you. Do they have an art house in Florida?" he asked as he walked out the door.

I don't know, Johnny, but they should. There should be an Art House or its equivalent on every corner in every city.

What can you do to stem the growing tide of violence among children? Let's try this: invest in children. Tithe your time; give a few hours a week to volunteering at an afternoon or Saturday program. Children need mentors, people who give them a reason to get up in the morning. Don't worry about duplicating services when it comes to children. We cannot have enough safe places for children to go. "Nothing you do for children is ever wasted," said Garrison Keillor. Let's believe him.

One more thing: it breaks my heart to see nine and ten year olds acting way beyond their years. When their conversations are filled with sexual innuendo, when their mouths are foul and violent, when they swagger and dress street tough, I can forget that these are only children. But to see these streetwise kids get excited about elementary school poems like "Mice" by Rose Flyman and "Sick" by Shel Silverstein and "Sometimes I Feel This Way" by John Ciardi, to hear them giggle and play, is to rediscover innocence—theirs and mine.

"The catcher in the rye" is what seventeen-year-old Holden Caulfield tells his little sister he wants to be, rejecting her suggestions of lawyer or scientist. Holden, the narrator and main character in J. D. Salinger's classic novel, *The Catcher in the Rye*, wants to preserve innocence. He tells his sister that he imagines thousands of small children playing in a field of rye. At the edge of the field is a cliff, and if the children wander too close and fall, he would be there to catch them.

I confess that an adolescent Holden still lives in this aging body. I know we can't protect children forever. But, my God, can we at least wait until they are teenagers before we leave them alone to fly off the cliffs of innocence? Can we at least try to catch them before they drop into the abyss of sex and drugs and violence? Anyone for a "catcher in the rye" movement?

Iraq War

"You are a monk," wrote Wayne Teasdale, "if upon awakening your first thought is of God." In other words, it doesn't matter if you live in a monastery; you are a monk if your heart is centered on God.

So what is a monk to do in times like this? What is a monk to do when the government calls for war and killing? What is a monk to do when bombs stand ready to kill the innocent and the monk is thinking always of God?

Thomas Merton, the world-renowned Trappist monk, asked the same question during the Vietnam War. He concluded that because war was a manifestation of a spiritual crisis, it "professionally concerns us as monks." He continued: "One of the basic elements in a monastic outlook in life is a respect for life, a respect for the living and growing things that God has created. . . . The monk's orientation should always be towards peace."

So, what is a monk to do in time of war? "Stop all the killing. . . . That's what a monk ought to be able to say in a war," Merton concluded. "If in a war a monk says 'Keep up the killing' then she or he is not a monk. When people are being killed a monk should be able to stand up and say, 'Let's see if we can get by without killing all these people. . . . In the name of truth this is wrong. In the name of God this should not be done.'"

I thought of Merton's call to stand up and be counted when four hundred of us gathered in downtown Erie to say "stop the killing," to say no to the bombing of Iraq. There were many old monks in the gathering, people whose lives are God-oriented and who look upon war as a spiritual crisis. These monks have marched against war and preparations for war for almost forty years. These monks keep showing up every time we decide to bomb the poor, whether in El Salvador, Nicaragua, Afghanistan, or Iraq. These monks stand up and are counted every time we add to the $100 million spent in the United States each day on weapons of war.

But for many of the two hundred college students who gathered to march, pray, chant, and speak for peace, it was a new "monk" moment, a life-altering moment, a stepping out of the crowd to take a stand against killing, to speak in the name of God. Their chants were brash and fresh; their talks were uplifting and poignant, full of the zeal of new vision and impossible dreams. I'm sure many of the old monks remembered the first stirring in their own hearts when they set out years ago to make the world a kinder, more compassionate place.

I know an old monk, a priest actually, who was recently removed from the pulpit of a diocesan cathedral in the South for telling the faithful that the cross takes precedence over the flag. The chancellor told him that the cross and flag are equal, that they work together. Imagine that. God's word and the White House form our consciences and set the course for life's choices. Imagine that, dear Jesus: Caesar and you, partners in life's meaning.

You are a monk, remember, if upon awakening your first thought is of God. If you are a monk, you have only one thing to do in time of war. You must stand up and say over and over again: "Stop the killing. In the name of God, stop the killing."

J

Joy

"Sometimes our light goes out, but is blown again into flame by an encounter with another human being. Each of us owes the deepest thanks to those who have rekindled this light," wrote Albert Schweitzer. The profundity of the quotation makes me leap automatically to an encounter with a great soul. And certainly in my lifetime, brushing shoulders with a Dan Berrigan, a Joan Chittister, a Cesar Chavez, a Dorothy Day has had this effect.

But would you believe a light being rekindled by a six-year-old boy? He came into my life as unexpectedly as Isaac to Sarah or John to Elizabeth. Except that a police siren, not an angel, announced the coming of abused and damaged Jimmy.

He came into my home with his mother and three brothers, fleeing a violent man and in need of safety. He lived with us for a while, and then we found the family a home in our inner-city neighborhood. He came at a time when I was so absorbed in self-pity and despair that self-centeredness could have easily swallowed me whole.

He certainly didn't look like a gift from the gods: prone to raging temper tantrums; slow in school; diagnosed as suffering from attention deficit disorder. As if that diagnosis explains a little boy who crawls behind furniture and shouts: "I hate myself. I want to kill myself."

How I loved this boy. How I wanted to be a big sister to him (well, closer to being a big grandmother). It looked like I was reaching out with a magnanimous heart, but he was really holding me up, giving me purpose and a reason to greet the morning sun. And slowly, slowly, Jimmy led me on the journey from self-absorption to presence, to attentiveness to another human being. Is there a journey more important in life?

It is easy to do good works, to practice charity, but it is difficult to be really present to another. At least it is for me. I may look like I'm there, but I am mentally impatient. Sometimes I am with a person who is talking to me and I reach for a phone to call someone else or page through my calendar for the next appointment. Sometimes I look like I'm listening to another but in my head I'm planning an article that I'm going to write. The person's concerns or needs don't seem that important compared to my time line. How I lust after what Simone Weil called the virtue of attentiveness. Why? Because I know it's the mark of sanctity.

To be fully present to another means setting aside our own agenda for a while and entering compassionately into the needs of another. To be lovingly attentive to another means transcending self and our need to be the center of the universe.

Attentiveness to the other—that is what Jimmy is teaching me. When I curl up on the couch to watch my favorite TV program and he calls—"Can I come over for homework help?"—I practice attentiveness. When my calendar says I should go to the office on Saturday morning and finish a proposal, but Jimmy wants to go fishing—I practice being present. And I can't fake it with him.

There are rewards, of course. After four years of tantrums; of trips to psychologists, allergists, social workers; of crawling after him behind sofas and under tables to talk and talk and repeat again and again, "I love you, Jimmy. I care about you." After four years of rejected hugs, he came into my study one afternoon and handed me a homemade valentine on which he had scrawled, "I like your help and love for me." Now isn't that worth a lifetime?

Jury Duty

"I asked the lawyer if he ever read Shakespeare" is how my dad greeted me when I joined him for our weekly Lake Erie perch dinner at the Polish Falcons Club.

"We put the water on when we saw you come in the door," Betty said as she poured our beer. Being a frequent diner at the Polish Falcons has its privileges. I get boiled pierogi even though the menu only offers fried.

"Well, the lawyer looked at me like I lost my mind," my dad continued, "but I wanted him to know why I can't serve on a jury. So I quoted from Shakespeare, 'Mercy is an attribute of God and we are most like God when mercy seasons justice.' I remembered a couple of lines from Cicero on the nature of justice, too. But I only remembered that from translating it in school and that was sixty years ago, so I didn't want to chance it. With Shakespeare I was sure. Anyway, I looked the lawyer straight in the eye and said, 'I would always choose mercy over justice. Justice is so arbitrary, but compassion is a constant.' The lawyer thanked me for coming and said to sign out with the court clerk.

"But just between you and me, sweetheart," my dad explained, "this case was a real stinker. Some poor guy involved in a car accident was up against an insurance company. They had these two big-time lawyers arguing the company's case." He took a long swig of Iron City and chuckled, "Besides, sweetheart, the guy was Polish."

"Oh, the guy was Polish," I laughed. "Then it's impossible for him to be guilty, isn't it?" He gave me a beaming smile and raised his beer glass. "Nazdrowie," he said. I clinked the glass and answered, "Nazdrowie." The unspoken toast was, "I taught you well, daughter."

Actually one of the most important things my dad taught me was encapsulated in that story. I'm talking about the journey of understanding God as mercy, not judgment. "I would always choose mercy over judgment," he told the lawyer. And I was there when he did.

When my brother returned from Vietnam, he moved back into my parents' house and began leading what they considered a rather loose life. Although my parents were patient, my mother finally decided some action was needed, and I was summoned home to discuss the matter over dinner.

Looking back, I guess everything in a Polish household was celebrated, mourned, or discussed in the context of delicious homemade meals. Somehow, food prepared with loving care made tragedy and death easier to handle, added to the warmth and joy of weddings, birthdays, and graduations, and in times of trouble reminded us that the bonds formed over daily meals gave strong and unshakable support. Anyway, we were finishing one of my mother's specialties, *golumki* (stuffed cabbage), when she said: "Maybe we should ask him to leave, Eddie. The relatives and neighbors are talking. How else will he know that we don't approve?"

My dad put down his fork and said in a soft voice: "He is our son, Mary. No matter what he does, he is still our son. And as long as we're alive, this will be his home."

Of all the faces of God that I have glimpsed in life, the clearest reflection is the one I saw in my dad that evening over dinner. I figure most children don't get from their parents that clear an example of how God is.

I think, too, that the best description Jesus gave of God was in the parable of the prodigal son. It is the story of a God who doesn't make sense. It is a tale of love without limits. It is a narrative poem about a God that Thomas Merton described as "mercy within mercy within mercy."

It is the spinning of a love song about a God who not only forgives and embraces and throws a feast for a returning child, but a God wild with love. This God even puts rings on our fingers when we don't deserve them. What largesse, what extravagance, what foolishness of heart.

I will probably search the rest of my days to become like the God I now adore, the God of "mercy within mercy within mercy." But thanks to my father, I have a memory that it is possible.

Justice

I was probably nine years old. My mother packed a lunch of braunschweiger sandwiches for my brother and me to take on a picnic with four other neighbor kids. The park was about three blocks from where we lived. It had a pitcher's mound and real bases, and we planned to play a few innings of baseball and then go to the picnic area and have lunch. How grown up we felt, old enough to leave our block and go on a picnic by ourselves. It was a big day.

We were in the middle of our ballgame when a gang of teenage boys came by. They grabbed our baseball bat and told us to leave the field so they could play. When I protested, they shoved me aside and grabbed our lunch bags—the braunschweiger sandwiches my mother had prepared so carefully—and they stomped up and down on them until the sandwiches were nothing but mush. I remember with certainty that it was braunschweiger because I hated braunschweiger, and yet I stood on the baseline and cried as if they were destroying the most precious thing I owned.

It was a mean-spirited and senseless action and I was powerless. My only recourse: tears and sobs. There was no one to help, no good Samaritan to intervene, no bigger kids to stand up to the bullies.

I never forgot how it felt to stand there helpless. I think the stomped braunschweiger sandwiches tendered my heart forever toward the weak and powerless, toward the innocent victim.

As the years went by it became impossible for me to just stand by and watch the innocent suffer needlessly at the hands of bullies, whether in government, corporations, or the military. Because of my education, my gifts, my position, I can do much more now than stand on the sidelines and cry.

The point is: Do I do all I can? Do I do all in my power to help, to intervene, to confront the institutional bullies face to face without becoming a bully myself?

Kindness

"Kindness and truth shall embrace" is one of my favorite psalm verses. But it's a love scene I find difficult to imagine. I remember struggling with the image when in the 1970s Bishop Matthiesen of Amarillo, Texas, issued a statement denouncing the decision of President Reagan to build a neutron bomb and calling upon workers in his diocese who worked in the nuclear plant, Pantex, to consider resigning. I rejoiced in his prophetic act—a historical first for the church.

Then I read an interview in a newspaper with one of the workers at Pantex, Robert Gutierrez, a Mexican American who was a deacon in his parish. He told the reporter: "This job is the first good thing I ever had. I quit school after the fourth grade to help support my family, but later earned a GED. . . . If the church thought my job was immoral, why wasn't something said seven years ago when I applied to the diaconate program?" Gutierrez says he can't sleep at night because he has a family to support and he feels trapped.

How can kindness and truth embrace here? Well, for starters, Gutierrez could quit his job and the Diocese of Amarillo could provide a pastoral program for Gutierrez, retraining, and a weekly check for him until he finds another job.

But Gutierrez is one person with one paycheck. Can the diocese do the same for all five hundred Catholics employed at Pantex? How about the tens of thousands involved in the nuclear industry across the country: scientists, engineers, and assembly workers? And that's only one sinful situation. What about all the other organizations that violate human rights?

I remember a scripture discussion with my peace community on a passage from Isaiah in which the prophet wrote that rain and snow do not return to the heavens "till they have watered the earth, making it fertile and fruitful." The community garden was just giving birth to a tomato crop, and we were full of nature imagery about how the soft summer rains had broken up the caked earth and enabled the seeds to grow. We contrasted such nourishing rains with the hard and sudden downpours that often flood the ground and drown the seed. Then someone in the group asked, "Are we as peacemakers so intent and intense about our truths regarding injustices that we are like the hard rain and cause more harm than good by trying to force growth when the ground is not ready?"

All of us could relate to the metaphor of trying to clear a straight path for the Lord with dynamite and a bulldozer instead of a pail of water and a hand shovel.

It made me think again of Robert Gutierrez. It made me think of all the victims of the "truth-filled" statements the church makes about abortion, homosexuality, divorce, and so forth. I imagine all the struggling people caught in sinful situations that they can't break away from. I imagine you and me. Maybe our only prayer should be, "Let my passion for truth always bend to kindness."

When he was a wise old man, Aldous Huxley wrote, "It's a bit embarrassing to have been concerned with human problems all one's life and find at the end that one has no more to offer by way of advice than 'try to be a little kinder.'"

John Lennon

I visited the John Lennon exhibit when it was on display in 2001 at the Rock and Roll Hall of Fame in Cleveland. It was a moving tribute to a creative genius and a testimony to his pursuit of peace, love, and imagination. Along with handwritten lyrics, original drawings, and displays of personal memorabilia, there was a wishing tree at the exhibit. Guests were asked to write a wish and hang it on the tree: "I wish we would give peace a chance, John." "I wish our government had your imagination, John." And then, this one, swinging from the branch, "I wish Yoko Ono were dead." It stopped me cold, ripped the joy from an afternoon spent with hope. How can a person walk through three floors of tribute to human possibility and end up with hate?

When the security guard wasn't looking, I grabbed that slip of paper and slipped it into my pocket. Enough. Blame me for censorship if you wish, but I will no longer expose children to messages of hate and despair. It was the least I could do for John Lennon. It was the least I could do to pay tribute to imagination, poetry, and possibility.

Once I heard a taped interview with Lennon on the radio, a section of which I copied into my journal. He was asked why he devoted so much energy to peace. Wasn't that a waste of time? Lennon replied that it was Leonardo da Vinci who made flying possible by projecting it, by bringing it into people's consciousness as a possibility. "What a person projects will eventually happen," Lennon said. "Therefore I always want to project peace. I want to put the possibility of peace into the public imagination."

In *The Prophetic Imagination* Walter Brueggeman writes: "The church must be a poetic community. A poetic community that offers explosive, concrete, subversive, critical images around which people can reorganize their lives."

We are desperate for poetry, for that which surprises and liberates us, opens our minds to new possibilities, that nurtures hope beyond cynicism, that frees us and evokes a new social reality.

In a time of "war on terrorism," when public images—in the media, in government, in sports, in the churches—center on revenge, death, violence, false patriotism, and fear, I hunger for a poetic, prophetic church that offers "explosive, concrete, subversive, critical images around which people can reorganize their lives."

Logic

I remember being in a seminar on nonviolence in which one of the participants, the daughter of a career Marine officer, talked of her struggle to reconcile violence with the message and life of Jesus. "I always looked upon the military position, the recourse to violence as logical," she said. Then one day it occurred to her that hell was logical; it made sense to be punished for what we'd done on earth. Heaven, she decided, was illogical. So were forgiveness, mercy, and compassion. The young woman concluded: "I have no trouble accepting heaven. It should be the same with nonviolence. Both are illogical; both are leaps of faith."

Meditation

I'm a firm believer in the axiom that to have peace in our world we must first have peace within ourselves. Not that we should stop working for nuclear disarmament and trek off to a hermitage, but that we should work on both levels at once. Unfortunately, working for peace is so crucial that it's easy to give mere lip service to nurturing the inner person. A friend wrote recently: "We seem to be so perpetually involved in action that we don't really understand the need to act harmoniously from a calm inner center—and the actions that evolve are in many cases a need to speak so as not to listen to the silence. . . . I believe very much that only a handful of people who act from that inner stillness will make a significant difference."

To develop inner stillness I am attracted to a method of meditation taught by the late Eknath Easwaran in his book *Meditation*. First, Easwaran asks us to find a favorite inspirational passage and memorize it. He recommends beginning with the prayer of Saint Francis, "Lord, make me an instrument of your peace. . . . " Once the passages is memorized, sit down, close your eyes, and slowly repeat it for about thirty minutes, concentrating on one word at a time, letting "the words slip one after another into the consciousness like pearls falling into a clear pond."

In case you're wondering why you should meditate, Easwaran reminds us that "we become what we meditate on."

Or, as the Buddha said, "All that we are is the result of what we have thought." Thus Easwaran recommends using a positive passage for meditation, one that bears the imprint of deep, personal, spiritual experience, one that is life-affirming and "returns you to the world and equal to its challenge." Although I've tried a number of meditation techniques, I stay with Easwaran because I love to have beautiful and inspiring words floating leisurely from head to heart. In my younger days I used to memorize poems, prayers, and scripture passages that I wanted to be bone of my bone, but for some reason—laziness, I guess—I stopped. Now I have a whole notebook full of sacred words that I will soon "know by heart."

Also, I've read enough prison literature to know that those undergoing great trial often credit their survival to repeating memorized prayers or poems or scripture to themselves. Fred Morris, an American missionary arrested in Recife, Brazil, recalls lying on a prison floor listening to his best friend scream in agony while being tortured. Morris writes:

> As I lay on the floor, feeling the unreality of it all, I found myself very self-consciously and deliberately repeating Psalm 23. It wasn't that I thought God was going to come down and deliver me, but it was reassuring to know that he was with me. . . . I kept reminding myself that there was more to me than anyone could touch. "Yea, though I walk through the valley of the shadow of death. . . . " They could kill me, but I wouldn't have to be afraid, because I was in God's hands. I found it a tremendous source of tranquility.

Mentor

Yesterday I buried Berrigan, my dog, my friend of sixteen years. A car hit her when I was already in bed. One of the sisters I live with often would let her out when she signaled the need by barking and leaping.

No one heard a car slam on its brakes. No one heard her yelp in pain. She was found in front of the neighbor's house, quite a distance from the street. Lynn went to get her and said it appeared that her spine was severed, her body was so twisted. However, there were no cuts, no bruises, no blood. When we brought her in the house, we laid her on her chair. She looked as we've seen her thousands of times, asleep, very peaceful. All of us cried at the memory service when we prayed, placed her body in a box, carried it in procession, and buried her in the backyard surrounded by flowers.

I am grateful to my only pet for many things, but especially for making me more comfortable with touch. I'm still not as spontaneous as I'd like, but it was Berrigan that I could cuddle and kiss and hold without fear of rejection.

Community retreat started today, and the leader said to spend the day thinking about those unlikely Christ figures in our lives who have helped redeem and re-create us. In a real way Berrigan helped me to greater wholeness. Tukaran, the beloved Indian poet who lived from 1608 to 1649, considered the most influential figure in the development of Marathi literature, expressed the same idea in his poem "First He Looked Confused":

> I could not lie anymore
> so I started to call
> my dog "God."

> First he looked,
> confused,
> then he started smiling,
> then he even danced.

> I kept at it:
> now he doesn't even
> bite.

> I am wondering if this
> might work on
> people?*

---

*From the Penguin anthology *Love Poems from God*, copyright 2002 Daniel Ladinsky and used with his permission.

Merton

I'm not ashamed to admit that I'm a Merton groupie. I keep his picture in my copybook and read whatever of his I can get my hands on. He has been a steady companion on my peace and justice journey. Here are some of my favorites.

Favorite book: The Sign of Jonas. I'm a pushover for journals, so that's one reason for choosing this book. But mostly I bring a lot of nostalgia to this choice. I can still picture myself—a white-veiled novice (very holy, I might add) walking in the convent yard, reading *The Sign of Jonas* and soaking up every word, much like the bare ground was absorbing the snowflakes falling lightly that December morning in 1969. Get the picture? This was heaven, I thought, being "alone with God in the quiet." I was a poster nun for *Monastic Digest.*

Ironically, it is this romantic and false sense of monasticism that Merton started to question in *The Sign of Jonas.* He had begun to realize that a true monk is not "separated from the world" but intimately united with all humankind, that the monastic vocation is predominantly a social one. At eighteen I didn't have enough experience to understand the spiritual development taking place in Merton, but the book gave me a deep appreciation for the importance of silence and solitude in the spiritual life.

The passage, however, that engraved itself on my heart is part of Merton's journal entry for Christmas morning, 1947:

> Outside the fields are full of hard frost. It
> was cold in bed last night and I went to
> sleep with the hymn of Lauds in my
> heart:
> "He did not despise the manger
> Nor did he refuse to sleep in straw.
> And he who does not permit the smallest
> bird to go hungry
> Was himself nourished with a little milk."

That image was all I thought about on Christmas 1969, and I began to identify more with the humanity of Jesus. Little by little, the pious "out of this world" novice began to disappear and in her place came a person who cared that the smallest child not be permitted to go hungry.

Most influential book: Thomas Merton on Peace. In 1971 I was doing volunteer work for the Harrisburg 7 Defense Committee—the group defending those accused of plotting to kidnap Henry Kissinger and blow up heating tunnels in the Pentagon. During the trial I lived with a friend who owned a trailer. After a day of exciting peace work—licking stamps, folding leaflets, collating press releases—I would go home and cuddle up on the couch with a book, a collection of Merton's writing on peace, edited by Gordon Zahn. Here was a comprehensive, spiritual, and rational discussion of the topics I had just started to become interested in: Catholic social teaching, just-war theory, nuclear pacifism, the nuclear-arms race, nonviolence, and Christian witness in the nuclear age. Zahn, a sociologist and longtime leader in the Catholic peace movement, believes that Merton's most lasting contribution to Catholic teaching on war and peace will be his writings on the theory and practice of nonviolence. I agree. For me, this book was an awakening to the moral ramifications of modern war. But it was much more than that. It awakened in me a lifelong search for and commitment to nonviolence.

Most inspiring act: Thomas Merton's underground letters. In 1961–62 Merton's superiors forbade him to write about peace because "it was not a monastic thing to do." Merton wrote under a pseudonym for periodicals like the *Catholic Worker* and carried on an extensive correspondence with peace movement people who circulated the letters. Here's one of my favorites, written to Daniel Berrigan:

> Look, a lot of the monastic party line we are getting ends up being pure unadulterated crap. In the name of lifeless parchment we are told that our life consists in pious meditations on scriptures and withdrawal from the world. Try

anything serious and immediately you get the word "activist" thrown at you. I have been told that I am destroying the image of the contemplative vocation when I write about peace. Even after *Pacem in Terris* when I reopened the question, I was told: "That is for the bishops, my boy." In a word, it is all right for the monk to break his ass putting out packages of cheese, and making a pile of money for the old monastery, but as to doing anything that is really fruitful for the Church that is another matter altogether.

The creativity of Merton's response to an order not to publish peace manuscripts is what I find inspiring. Although he complied with the order to cease submitting articles for publication, the letters still circulated and were influential in guiding and supporting the Catholic peace movement being birthed at that time.

Favorite passages: I have three. The first is Merton's moment of awakening on the corner of 4th and Walnut in Louisville, Kentucky. After years of withdrawal from the world in search of holiness, Merton is given the grace to see where true sanctity is found. He suddenly sees "the secret beauty" of each person's heart, "the person that each one is in God's eyes," and muses that if we saw ourselves and others that way, "I suppose the big problem would be that we would fall down and worship each other."

My second favorite passage is his mystical ode to rain, written from his hermitage: "The rain surrounded the cabin. . . . Think of it: all the speech pouring down, selling nothing, judging nobody, drenching the thick mulch of dead leaves, soaking the trees, filling the gullies. . . . What a thing it is to be absolutely alone in the forest at night, cherished by this wonderful, unintelligent, perfectly innocent speech, the most comforting speech in the world."

The third passage I return to every Christmas season for my lectio because it is, for me, the best theological commentary on the incarnation:

Into this world, this demented inn, in which there is no room for him at all, Christ has come uninvited. . . . His place is with those who do not belong, who are rejected by power because they are regarded as weak, those who are discredited, who are denied the status of persons, tortured and exterminated. With those for whom there is no room, Christ is personally present in this world. He is mysteriously present in those for whom there seems to be nothing but the world at its worst.

Well, I could go on. I have a favorite poem, a favorite essay, a favorite biography, a favorite anecdote, but it would be better if you compile your own list. God knows there are enough Merton books now to keep you busy a lifetime.

Mourning

"Blessed are they who mourn," the scripture reads, "for they shall be comforted" (Mt 5:4). But we must handle mourning with care. How we mourn pays tribute to how the deceased lived. A Hasidic teaching explains this clearly: "There are three ascending levels of how one mourns: With tears—that is the lowest. With silence—that is higher. And with song—that is the highest."

I saw this teaching take flesh during my mother's funeral.

It had been a heartbreaking week for the family. My mother went to the hospital for tests and within five days she was dead.

I had seen my father cry before; he is not the kind of man who is afraid or ashamed of tears. But he is also a disciplined man. For him, tears have their proper place; they flow for very private grief. Since I had spent the greater part of the week with him, I knew he was heartbroken, filled with almost unbearable sorrow. It surprised me that there were not tears at the funeral parlor or at mass. Tears I expected. I was not prepared for song.

I should have known better. My father's deepest expression of love is song. I have cherished memories of being carried for hours in my father's arms as he filled the house with "Let Me Call You Sweetheart" or "Down by the Old Mill Stream." His favorites, however, were Polish hymns. He would sit in his armchair all afternoon and sing from the worn *Spiewniczek* (Polish hymnal).

So it shouldn't have surprised me that when the funeral Mass ended and we started to move my mother's casket down the aisle, my father broke into song. Though there were tears in his eyes, his voice filled the church, drowning out the choir and the mourners with his favorite prayer, "Serdeczna Matko," a hymn to the Mother of God that captures the soul of Poland.

It was a moment suspended in time: the church bells pealing, some in the congregation crying, and my father, walking slowly behind the casket, singing farewell to his wife of forty-three years, paying a profound tribute to my mother and the love they shared.

That day I learned something about the depth of mourning.

Mystic Resister

In ancient days people would go to the desert to find a "holy one." The disciple would seek out these desert fathers and mothers and ask for a "word," a teaching that gave some insight into the ways of God.

I found a holy one when I went to the Nevada desert for the Pax Christi Witness at the nuclear test site located there. I was led to her hermitage by Sister Mary Jo Leddy, who directed the day of prayer and reflection prior to our action. Mary Jo suggested that we consider Etty Hillesum the patron saint of resistance. She gave a reason, too. Etty, she said, resisted out of gratitude.

I was familiar with Hillesum, having read *An Interrupted Life: The Diaries of Etty Hillesum*. To read the intimate journals of Etty, a young Dutch Jewish woman who died in Auschwitz, is to meet someone "grasped by God."

All the criteria for sanctity is found in her diaries. One is struck by the asceticism, the resistance to self-deception, the ruthless honesty with self that permits no half-truths, the love affair with God that grows more passionate each day, and the heroic love for others.

The two loves—God and people—are inseparable, and it comes as no surprise that one so afire with God spent her final days bringing comfort to those awaiting death at a concentration camp in Westerbork, Holland. Etty mirrors love's labor: giving of self with abandon, though there is no consolation, no hope of good results, and no end in sight. Given an opportunity to leave Holland, she refused to forsake the others and joined them on a train to Auschwitz. What is there to say about diaries that end: "I have broken my body like bread and shared it out. . . . And why not, they were hungry and had gone without for so long."

William James once said of saints, "It is not possible to be quite as mean as we naturally are when they have passed before us." If this is a legitimate criterion, then Etty Hillesum is a saint. I closed her journals with a deep sense of reverence, certain I was holding a sacred text.

So I guess I've always considered Etty a saint—I've seen in her life the meaning of God. What I've been thinking about since Nevada, however, is naming Etty the patron saint of resistance because she resisted out of gratitude.

That makes all the difference, of course. I've met people who resisted out of anger, out of conviction, out of guilt, out of self-righteousness, out of self-need, out of peer pressure. But those who resisted out of gratitude for life are few. What a treasure, though, when you discover them.

On each page of her journal you find Etty struggling to accept life as gift, to break free of the illusion that we are in ultimate control of our own life or the lives of others. The slow and painful journey toward the self-knowledge necessary for true inner freedom is one from which Etty never wavers. And she achieves it:

I don't feel in anybody's clutches; I feel safe in God's arms
. . . and no matter whether I'm sitting at this beloved old
desk now or in a bare room in the Jewish district or perhaps in a labor camp under SS guards in a month's time—
I shall always feel safe in God's arms. They may well suc-
ceed in breaking me physically, but no more than that. I
may face deprivation and cruelty, the likes of which I cannot imagine. . . . Yet all that is as nothing compared to
the immeasurable expanse of my faith in God and my
inner receptiveness.

Early in her diary Etty states her goal in life by quoting
from a poem by Verwey: "'Melodious rolls the world from
God's right hand.' I, too, want to roll melodious out of God's
hand." We call these "melodies of God" the pure of heart. In
a sense they are always in a posture of worship, of adoration,
of thanksgiving. Just as the Beatitudes promise, the pure of
heart see God. They see God everywhere and in everyone.
Consequently, the only possible response for the grateful is
resistance. Those in awe of the gift of life must resist the manu-
facture of death in all its forms.

Etty Hillesum was transformed into ultimate resistance. She
writes an imaginary conversation to a friend: "Yes, life is beautiful and I value it anew at the end of every day, even though I
know the sons of mothers . . . are being murdered in concentration camps. . . . Do not relieve your feelings through hatred, do not seek to be avenged on all German mothers, for
they, too, sorrow at this very moment for their slain sons."
And in another journal entry, "I believe that I will never be
able to hate any human being for their so-called 'wickedness,'
that I shall only hate the evil that is within me." To refuse to
return hatred is to break the cycle of violence. Etty did so in
her own body.

It's difficult, maybe impossible, to explain the mystic resister. Yet it is only the mystic resister who makes a difference.
To get a glimpse of what it means to resist out of gratitude, I
recommend the diaries of Etty Hillesum.

She is a good desert mother, with a "word" needed for these times. True, she may never be formally canonized as the patron saint of resistance. But you might want to do so in your heart.

Thich Nhat Hanh

The Russian mystic Saint Seraphim writes, "If you have inner peace, thousands of people around you will be saved." In my lifetime, I've met about a half dozen people who fit the saint's description. And each encounter has intensified my hunger for the bread that gives such wholeness.

One of those people is Thich Nhat Hanh, the Buddhist monk, poet, and best-selling author. During the Vietnam War he led the nonviolent resistance movement in South Vietnam and was forced to flee the country. After the truce was signed, the Communist government would not permit him to return, and he lives in exile in France on a small farm where he has a small Buddhist community. In the late 1970s I interviewed him for a book on monasticism and the peace movement. At the time he was still trying to settle Vietnamese refugees and other victims of the war.

Here was a man who had every right to be agitated, preoccupied, in a constant hurry; his life was a horror-movie serial. Daily he received anguished letters from friends telling of imprisonment, hunger, illness, and death. Yet never had I met a more peaceful person. Whenever I think of him, swinging in a tire swing in the backyard of his small Sweet Potato Community in France, I can feel the peace of his presence.

Besides becoming a very popular author, Nhat Hanh is a much-sought-after lecturer and retreat leader. He has done exceptional work with forgiveness, love, and reconciliation retreats for U.S. veterans damaged in the Vietnam War. I couldn't help but think of the quotation by Saint Seraphim when I recently read his *Teachings on Love.* In the book he recounts a story told by a veteran during a retreat. The veteran said that during the war, guerrillas killed an entire platoon of his friends. To retaliate, the survivors baked cookies, put explosives in them, and left the cookies on the roadside. When some Vietnamese children saw the cookies, they ate them and the explosives went off. The children died in agony in their parents' arms. The image of these little ones suffering after the explosives ignited their small stomachs was so deeply ingrained on the veteran's heart that, twenty years later, he still could not sit in the same room with children.

I try to imagine myself leading a retreat like this. What could I possibly say or be to this person? That's how I know that I don't have the inner peace of Nhat Hanh. Someone as centered as he is knows what each person needs. Nhat Hanh told the veteran to "begin anew."

"You killed five or six children that day," Nhat Hanh said. "Can you save the lives of five or six children today? You still have your body, you still have your heart; you can do many things to help children who are dying in the present moment."

And just as Saint Seraphim predicted, the veteran responded to this man of inner peace and was healed.

Night

When Robert Louis Stevenson was a little boy, he lived in a house on a hillside in Scotland. Every evening he would watch the lamplighter walk through the streets in the valley below, lighting each of the village street lights. "Look, Mother," he would say. "Here comes the man who punches holes in the darkness."

I've had many lamplighters walk through my life and punch holes in my darkness. Here is one of them.

I was sixteen before I had the courage to sneak into my first non-Catholic religious service. It was a revival meeting under a big tent in a vacant lot, two blocks from my house.

Four high school friends and I went under cover of night, conscious that we were flirting with the dangers of everlasting fire—remember, in the 1950s it was a mortal sin for Catholics to attend non-Catholic services. We sat with superior smirks while the preacher ranted and raved about the evil tobacco weed and his every sentence was met with foot stomping and clapping and "Amen, Brother, amen."

But when Sister Woods began to describe her celestial visit, her ride in the flaming chariot with Elijah, it was too much. Try as we might—pressing our nostrils together, biting our lips—we could not contain our giggles. And just as Sister Wood was being swept into the bosom of Jesus and the sax wailed and the drummer picked up tempo and the congregation was on its feet swaying and wailing, the five of us rushed for the exit.

"Boy, are they ever stupid," I laughed. "Amen, Sister, alleluia," answered my friend Pat.

I don't know why I returned, but I did. The next evening I found myself in the back of the tent watching. It was early, but already about twenty people were seated on the long, backless benches. I noticed that they were dressed poorly and recognized some faces from the night before.

Just as the Angelus bells began to ring at my parish church, the preacher picked up the microphone. "To begin the meeting, will you all rise and greet your neighbor? Shake hands and welcome each other. And let us sing out our joy."

The little band started playing, and people stood, marched around the tent, shook hands, and sang "Oh, When the Saints Go Marching In." I dug the toe of my sneaker into the dirt and lowered my eyes, embarrassed at this open display of affection at a religious service. Remember, we're talking pre–Vatican II here, when people did not even dare talk to their neighbors in a Catholic church, let alone greet each other with a kiss of peace.

I looked up just in time to see a man, toothless and grinning, approaching me, his hand extended. Our eyes met. I remembered my snickers from the previous night. Quickly, I turned and stepped through the tent flap—shamed.

Up to the revival experience, I had a closed mind about religion. I was in darkness. I thought all non-Catholics were spiritually inferior. Because of that brief encounter with this open and welcoming man, I looked upon other religions, other expressions of piety, with greater openness.

A Hasidic tale tells about an old rabbi who asked his pupils how they could tell when the night had ended and the day had begun. Then he answered his question: "It's when you can look upon the face of any man or woman and see that it is your brother or sister. Because if you cannot see this, it is still night."

The toothless man in the revival tent was one of my lamplighters. He punched holes in the darkness and brought me light.

Numbness

When I was working as a journalist for the local paper, the city editor sent me to interview a man who had multiple sclerosis. He was a brilliant draftsman for a major corporation when the disease struck. He could no longer go to work and planned to do some drafting at home to support his wife and children. He was hoping a newspaper feature would interest local businessmen, who might throw a bone or two his way.

While he was telling me his story, he suddenly broke down and began to sob. Then he spat these words at me: "Why did they send you? You're too young to understand what's happening to me. You don't know what it's like to have a life fall apart. You can never write my story."

After a few minutes, he regained control and we continued the interview. I was moved by the encounter, of course, and wrote what I considered a strong and compassionate feature. I tried to capture how this man was holding on to a thread of hope, how he didn't want to call it quits at the age of forty, how he didn't want charity but only a chance to put meaning into his life.

I handed the finished copy to the city editor. She glanced at it and said: "Another story about a cripple. We just ran one last week." Then she threw it into the wastebasket.

When the paper came out that afternoon, I looked at the inches of newsprint given to filler stories, to copy that really belonged in TV and movie magazines—such trivia compared to one man's future.

I recall this story because today an appeal letter for the people of Haiti came across my desk. I glanced at the return address and said to myself: "Another cry for help. I gave to the poor last week." Then I tossed it in the trash.

Obscenity

One of the most obscene pictures in today's world is a person eating out of a garbage can. When I was in London once, I sat on a bench in the square outside Westminster Cathedral right in front of a McDonald's. A woman approached the garbage can, rummaged through it, and pulled out a few french fries, which she ate. My friend and I stared at her and discussed whether to give her some money. She was obviously a shopping-bag lady, probably in her mid fifties, poorly dressed, wearing two different kinds of shoes. While we were discussing how to respond, the lady disappeared.

The scene had its black humor. On one side of the street was the headquarters for the ESSO Oil Company; on the other side, the headquarters of the British Catholic Church; and between was McDonald's, the symbol of U.S. economic power. In the midst of these idols to economic and religious power was a woman eating out of a garbage can.

Feeling like a hypocrite, I went into the cathedral for a peace Mass being celebrated to end violence in Northern Ireland. The homily was on feeding the hungry. As I approached the altar for communion, I stepped back to make room for a woman to my left—and there she was—the street lady.

After the liturgy I approached her and said, "Pardon me, would it embarrass you if I offered you this money?" She grasped it like a leech. I've seen her eyes so many times among

Erie's poor. She's Adele, Polish Mary, Lee, Dicie, and thousands of other women worldwide who walk the streets and have a one-word vocabulary: *survival.*

One-pointed Attention

What does mindfulness or one-pointed attention have to do with nonviolence? Why practice mindfulness or one-pointed attention? The Hasidic teachers said it this way: There was once a preacher who repeated over and over, "Put God in your life, put God in your life." But the holy rabbi of the village said: "Our task is not to put God into our lives. God is already there. Our task is simply to realize that."

So we practice one-pointed attention to become more aware of the reality of God's abiding presence. And the more centered we are in God, the softer, less violent our hearts should become.

All of us have special or intense glimpses of this reality, times when each of us—in a special way—experienced communion with God. We call these peak experiences or core experiences or mystical experiences or contemplative moments. I always marvel at these encounters of God when I read about them or meet people who have experienced them.

A Vietnam vet was out on operation in the middle of the night, wading through mud and water from one little island to the next. He writes:

On one island we came to, there was one tree full of fireflies. I was in a whole atmosphere of death and destruction and depression and hopelessness, and all of a sudden I saw this tree lit up brighter than most Christmas trees—from fireflies! I wanted to drop to my knees. I just stood there with my mouth open like everybody else. But I wanted to drop on my knees and pray, "God, thanks for the sign." That helped me get through the rest of the period. It was a sign of life itself, a sign from life.

When I was leading a weekly prayer group, I asked the people to share a core or peak experience from their own lives. I used as an example a Bob Dylan concert that I had recently attended. I talked about Dylan singing "Blowin' in the Wind" and how the thousands of people there, many of them from the 1960s, joined him in singing that anthem of freedom and peace. I said that I felt lifted out of myself and united with all, that it was a taste of goodness and the reign of God on earth.

One of the women, Marlene, spoke up and said, "I don't know if this is what you mean but. . . . " Then she told us that when she was a younger woman, she had taken her children to the Lake Erie beach to swim. She sat on a blanket in the sand and, as was her custom, recited the Rosary as she watched her children play in the water. Without warning, her seventeen-year-old daughter began calling for help and, despite all her efforts, Marlene watched her daughter die right before her eyes. "I hated God," she told the group. "I hated God intensely for months. Then one night something washed over me," she said. "I heard a voice saying, 'I love you. I love you.' It forced me to my knees."

"I've been married twice," Marlene continued, "and I've loved each man intensely, but nothing in those two relationships came close to the love I experienced in the night. From that night on I have had absolutely no fear of death."

Then she looked at me and asked, "Is that what you mean by a peak experience?"

Sometimes these experiences are given to us because we need them to get through hard times. Sometimes they are given so that we will remember them in dry and dark times. Sometimes they are given as stepping stones for our spiritual journey. Sometimes they are given to make us more aware of the ordinary. Whatever the reason, they are pure gift.

Any good spiritual teacher will warn against looking for God only in the extraordinary. Core experiences, mystical experiences, moments of faith—we must let them come and go like any other experience. We also have to be careful not to let these experiences fool us into thinking that God is more present in them than in any other area of our lives. Remember the

Hasidic tale and remember that Jesus told us the reign of God is within us. Right here. Right now. All we have to do is become more aware of it. And the more we grow in awareness of that reality, the more nonviolent our heart becomes. If God is ever present in me . . . in you . . . in creation, then how can we hate? kill? destroy? The result of genuine spiritual training is to arrive at that day when we see the sacred in the simple, the extraordinary in the ordinary.

P

· ·

Passion

Alone in my office in late afternoon, I put my head down on the desk and cried. Nothing about monastic life had moved me to such depths in many years. What brought the tears was reading the last testament of Dom Christian de Chergé, OSCO, prior of our Lady of Atlas Monastery, Algeria, one of seven Trappists massacred by armed Islamic militants. After he and his monks were murdered, the document was released.

Why such tears? First, I was moved by the purity of Dom Christian's words. Before me, in print, was a living parable of someone who had found the treasure buried in a field. With disarming simplicity he spoke of love and forgiveness of enemies. Only one who has found the treasure can be filled with such inner stillness; only one holding the rare treasure can know such freedom. He wrote:

> If it should happen one day—and it could be today—
> that I become a victim of the terrorism which now seems
> to encompass all the foreigners living in Algeria, I would
> like . . . them to be able to associate this death with so
> many equally violent ones allowed to fall into anonym-
> ity. My life has no more value than any other. Nor any
> less value. I have lived long enough to know that I share
> in the evil which seems, alas, to prevail in the world and
> even in that which would strike me blindly.

Finally, this personal address to his assassin:

> And you, too, my last minute friend, who will not know
> what you are doing, yes, for you too I say this THANK YOU
> and A-DIEU—to commend you to the God in whose face
> I see yours. And may we find each other, happy "good
> thieves" in Paradise, if it please God.

I was also moved by the courage of Dom Christian's life. For
thirty years I've had a paperweight on my desk with this quotation from Daniel Berrigan: "Don't just do something, stand
there." Dom Christian and the Trappists stood there. They
stood there through threats, terror, and months of nightmares.
They stood there when others panicked and pleaded with them
to escape. They stood there, bearing witness, a sign of peace,
a place of prayer, a community of caring.

But there is more to the story of tears than being moved by
purity and courage. Like our dreams, our tears tell us something about ourselves. Joan Chittister writes: "Apathy is what
happens when there's no life left in the commitment. What
has no life for us renders us lifeless. The secret, of course, lies
in bringing to lost loves what they can no longer bring to us."

I think I wept that afternoon for a "lost love." I think I was
weeping for my "lost love," the monastic, the Christian life.
First love brings such passion. I could imagine myself as a
novice, even as a newly professed, giving the same testimony
as Dom Christian. But with the passing years ideals can shatter, or worse, dissipate amid petty community politics. Or private ambitions. Or personal dreams unfulfilled. Or just the
simple fatigue from the mundane. Rather than risk all for the
precious pearl, we settle for a cheap imitation, a glittering piece
of costume jewelry.

Then along comes Dom Christian and the six other
Trappists in Algeria to remind me that I once staked my life
on an all-or-nothing dice game and agreed to only one roll of
the dice. The seven martyrs of Algeria freely offer their lives
and show me how to bring back to a lost love what it can no
longer bring to me.

Their witness is clear: To bring passion back to our lives we must rid ourselves of the comfortable and place ourselves at risk. To bring passion back to our lives we must live on the edge, the margin, among the poor, in vulnerable and volatile places, steeping our days in prayer and forgiving love. A passionate Christian life is about giving our lives for something greater than ourselves.

"Ah, lost love," the Christian ideal pleads to us, "return to me with all your heart."

Pax Christi

Pax Christi, the Catholic peace movement, was born in a prison—and not just any prison, but a prison filled with men whose destination was the concentration camp at Buchenwald.

It was World War II, and France was occupied by Germany. Herded together in a French state prison were French resistance fighters and others, including priests and religious, who had harbored hunted Jews. One of the resistance fighters asked a fellow prisoner, Bishop Theas, to celebrate Mass.

Bishop Theas was in prison for nonviolent resistance. He had condemned, through a pastoral letter, the persecution of the Jews, the deportation of French workers to Germany for forced labor, and the reprisal destruction of whole villages.

The prison was seething with hatred and anger. Only five weeks before an entire nearby village had been massacred. There, in retaliation for the killing of German occupation troops, the French inhabitants were herded into the village church and the church set afire.

Bishop Theas agreed to celebrate the prison Mass. He chose for his homily this theme: Love your enemy. He read to these brave, honorable, courageous French freedom fighters what they least expected: "Love your enemies, do good to them that hate you, and pray for those that persecute you."

Some of the prisoners interrupted the bishop. "The gospel is terrible," they said. "This gospel is impossible to live." Theas replied, "I cannot preach anything to you but what Jesus said, 'Love your enemies.'"

Then he led the prisoners in the prayer that Jesus taught. When he came to the line, "Forgive us our trespasses as we forgive those who trespass against us," he paused and added one word—*Germany.*

There was a moment of silence and then an explosion of grief and anger. "No, no," the prisoners shouted. Someone screamed, "But they've killed our children." We can only imagine the terrible pain and anguish. But Bishop Theas gently insisted that this was necessary. He repeated the word—*Germany.* Many could not finish the prayer. Some did. All understood, perhaps for the first time, the terrible implications of the words that Jesus taught us to pray.

Theas was finally released from prison, but the incident altered his life. Because of it he determined to devote the rest of his days to reconciliation efforts between France and Germany. When French lay Catholics organized a prayer crusade in behalf of the German people, Theas blessed the effort. This prayer crusade was the beginning of Pax Christi.

Pentecost

At Pentecost we pray, "Lord, send down your spirit and renew the face of the earth." When the daily headlines scream that vengeance and violence are the only valid responses to injuries, hurts and tales of horror, we need organizations like the Fellowship of Reconciliation, the oldest religious-based international peace organization, which over the years has presented story after story of unconditional forgiveness in the midst of unimaginable violence. The stories I have clipped from *Fellowship* and pasted in my scrapbook, as well as my heart, tell us that we need human faces of forgiveness to renew the earth.

We need the face of Magda Trocmé. During World War II, Magda was preparing supper when two men arrived to arrest her husband, André, for harboring Jews. André was on an errand, so the men had to wait. When it was time for the evening meal, Magda asked them to join her at the table along with the Trocmé children. "But how could you have such people at your table?" she was asked later. "It was meal time," she said, "and they also had to eat." As one of the men ate, he wept.

We need the face of an old Russian woman. The Soviet poet Yevtushenko recalls in his autobiography that when he was a child he was taken by his mother to Moscow to view the German war prisoners who were being marched through the streets in a single column. The streets were filled with hate-filled onlookers, mostly Russian women who had lost a father, husband, brother, or son to the Germans. The soldiers and policemen had all they could do to hold the women back. Yevtushenko writes:

> All at once the German soldiers appeared: thin, unshaven, wearing dirty blood-stained bandages, hobbling on crutches or leaning on the shoulders of their comrades; the soldiers walked with their heads down. The crowd became dead silent—the only sound was the shuffling of boots and the thumping of crutches.
>
> Then I saw an elderly woman in broken-down boots push her way through the police line and up to the column of soldiers. From inside her coat she unwrapped a crust of black bread and pushed it awkwardly into the pocket of a soldier. Suddenly, from every side, women came running toward the soldiers, pushing into their hands bread, cigarettes, whatever they had. The soldiers were no longer enemies. They were people.

We need the face of an old Salvadoran woman. She was visited by national guardsmen who had come to take her granddaughter away. The woman's sons had already been tortured and killed. While they waited for the granddaughter to return from an errand, she offered the guards water, saying to herself: "To give water to the thirsty is the most sacred thing in life. You cannot deny that, even to the most wicked for being wicked. There is not a drop of hypocrisy or servility in my offering. It is only offering what God himself would not deny the devil. . . . You mustn't consider it an act of kindness or commiseration. It's a simple act of humanity."

We need the face of Vedran Smailovic, the principal cellist of the Sarajevo Opera. During the siege of Sarajevo in 1992 a mortar shell exploded at four o'clock in the afternoon outside a bakery in the city where people had lined up to buy bread. Twenty-two people were killed and hundreds were wounded in the explosion, and yet the next day hungry people again came for bread. At exactly four o'clock Smailovic arrived in front of the bakery carrying a chair and cello and dressed in formal black suit and white tie. With great solemnity he sat down and played the mournful "Adagio" by Albinoni. Every day at the same time, for twenty-one consecutive days, Smailovic offered this gesture of hope and beauty to his war-torn city. The beautiful melody of Albinoni's "Adagio," wafting through rubble and death, was an audacious gesture that lifted the spirit and electrified the imagination of peoples around the world.

A teaching from the Jewish tradition goes like this: "If you are walking in a forest alone at night and another joins you with her lantern, then you can walk safely and joyfully together. But if you come to a crossroads and your friend departs with the lantern, then you must grope your way alone unless you carry a light within you." These are the faces of four people who carry lanterns that can light the dark forest of our times. And they carry a light within, a light we can all learn to make our own.

Pigeons

I like to think of pigeons as pets of the poor. Bag ladies share stale soup-kitchen bread with them; they are constant companions to the homeless who sleep on sidewalk grates; like the poor, they are shooed away from every public park and square. Wherever the poor are gathered, you will find flocks of pigeons.

And pigeons are so ordinary and commonplace that no one pays particular attention to them except to cuss them out. Reminds you of the poor, doesn't it?

In the short story "Pigeon Feathers" by John Updike, a young boy, David, who is struggling with life's meaning and God's existence, experiences a moment of epiphany by examining pigeons that he has just shot. It is the first time David has seen a bird this close, and he observes that

> across the surface of the feathers played idle designs of colors, no two alike, designs executed it seemed, in a controlled rapture . . . one broadly banded in slate shades of blue, another mottled all over in rhythms of lilac and gray. . . . The next was almost wholly white, but for a salmon glaze at its throat. As he stood up . . . he was robed in this certainty: that the God who had lavished such craft upon these worthless birds would not destroy His whole Creation by refusing to let David live forever.

There's the beauty and wonder of it: to discover the extraordinary in the ordinary. If you look, really look, at anything, even one pigeon, you will fall on your knees before its beauty. The same holds true for each person in the soup kitchen line. As one definition of contemplation attests, "It's a matter of taking a long, loving look at the real."

Prayer

Oh, I love to play the game of seeking God. I'm a spirituality "bookaholic." I'm a scripture journal fanatic. I have boxes of recipes for the perfect meditation style. I keep getting up earlier in the morning to find God, as if there is some secret formula connecting holiness with beating the rooster's crow. I get a real high walking into religious bookstores that smell of incense and have those fantastic Buddhist chants and gongs piped into the stereo system.

I own a prayer shawl, special prayer sandals, and three sets of prayer beads on which to recite my mantras. As a Benedictine sister, I've been present for about twelve thousand communal prayer sessions.

But I don't have a clue if I've ever said a prayer. The more addicted I get to all of these spiritual disciplines and artifacts, the less sure I am of what, if anything, they have to do with seeking God. But I still play along. It's the most fun I've had since I got too old to play basketball.

I exaggerate, of course. Put me on a lie-detector machine and ask me if these prayer aids and sessions have anything to do with seeking the Source of all being, and I'll tell you a story:

"Is there anything I can do to make myself Enlightened?" the seeker asked the elder. "As little as you can do to make the sun rise in the morning," the elder answered. "Then of what use are the spiritual exercises you pre-scribed?" the seeker asked. And the elder answered, "To make sure you are not asleep when the sun begins to rise."

It's as good a story as any to put your trust in when it comes to prayer.

Quality

I've read a lot of prayers in my life, but only a few haunt me in their honesty, simplicity, beauty, and tough love. The prayers that I return to again and again because of these qualities are by Teresa of Avila, Thomas Merton, Thomas à Kempis, Saint Augustine, Mary Stewart, Charles de Foucauld, and this one by Saint Vincent de Paul:

> You will find that charity
> is a heavy burden to carry,
> heavier than the kettle of soup
> and the basket of bread.
>
> But you must your gentleness
> and your smile keep.
>
> Giving soup and bread
> isn't all that you can do.
>
> The poor are your masters—
> terribly sensitive and exacting
> as you will see.
>
> But the more demanding they seem
> the more unjust and bitter
> the more you must give them your love.

It is only because of your love
only your love
that the poor will forgive you
the bread you give them.

Saint Vincent de Paul is no wimp, no naive romantic or do-gooder. He defended the rights of the poor and abandoned to such a degree in the seventeenth century that the church named him the patron of works of charity. That means he had lots of experience under his belt.

So the prayer he wrote about charity deserves attention. It's a tough one to pray, as are all prayers written by those who have been in the trenches. As a matter of fact, I choke on many of these lines, especially in the last stanza. Do we need to be forgiven by the poor for the bread we give them? You betcha.

The poor, you see, are not dumb. They know that we have no right to give them food. They know that food does not belong to us. It is not ours to give to them. They know—as Meister Eckhart said—"there is no such thing as 'my bread.' All bread is ours."

So when seventy-eight-year-old Evy stands for a couple of hours in the food-pantry line on Monday morning—in the sweltering sun, the bone-chilling rain, the blinding snow—to get a small bag of groceries, she has a right to spit in the face of the person handing her the food. She has a right to say, "You've stolen my food, and I've come to get it back."

But Evy doesn't. Instead, she tells us how much that meager bag of groceries means to her. To hear her describe it, you'd think Emmaus was like the prophet Elisha, who gave the poor widow a jar full of oil that never ran dry.

"I use one item at a time," Evy said. "I make Swedish meatballs with your rice. . . . I eat a slice of bread a day. . . . Yesterday there was little in the house and I went to your bag and, sure enough, there was still a small can of potatoes. Without this bag of groceries I couldn't get through the week."

According to Saint Vincent, we should be on our knees begging Evy's forgiveness. Instead, she thanks us. Let's hope that

Evy is so kind to us because she feels genuinely loved. Let's
hope.

Questions

First, the good news: guest musicians and artists who come
to the Inner-City Neighborhood Art House always express
amazement at the quality of questions and amount of "artis-
tic" knowledge the children possess. A recent guest conductor
from the Erie Philharmonic was no exception. He said that
the questions asked by Noah, an eight-year-old boy, were the
deepest he'd ever received from an audience of children.
    The bad news: Noah, the boy who asked the questions, is a
classic at-risk kid. He can't stay on task; he's disruptive in class;
he's always fighting; he's angry and lacks self-control. So you
can imagine how amazed the teachers were when he asked the
conductor, "How does sound vibrate?" And followed that question with, "What would the world be like without music?"
Why is this bad news? Because the overwhelming odds are
that Noah will never reach the potential that his questions
indicate.
    Unless, of course, we overwhelm Noah with the good news
of mentoring: the time, interest, support, and opportunity that
we give him.

    A teacher at an inner-city Catholic school in Cleveland no-
ticed a student who was unusually listless and inattentive in
class. So she asked him if he had eaten breakfast. He said, "It
wasn't my turn." After a few probing questions, she learned
that he had several brothers and sisters, and the family budget
only allowed the children to take turns eating breakfast. His
turn came three days a week, and today wasn't one of them.
Why, in the richest country in recorded history, do children
in some families have to take turns eating breakfast?

    At the Kids' Cafe children get a meal, tutoring help, gym
activities, and a chance to participate in an incentive program

for serving others. Children can earn Kids' Cafe dollars by doing extra cleaning, helping younger kids with homework, and taking leadership roles. Once a week they can redeem their "dollars" at the Kids' Cafe store for toys, candy, toiletries, books, or school supplies.

On the week before Christmas, eight-year-old Shaq handed his slip to the cashier and purchased eleven dollars worth of merchandise. The woman who manages the Kids' Cafe store looked at Shaq's slip and took it to the director. "Does this look right to you?" she asked. The director smiled. "No," she said, "Shaq only earned one dollar last week. He added the other "1" to make it "11.""

So Shaq was called to the office. When they opened his bag of purchases, what do you think they found? Cereal, shampoo, toilet paper, and soap. Not one piece of candy. Not one toy.

The director sat the boy down and told him that there was no need to lie. "Everything we have is for you," she said.

This story was told and retold. Most people sympathized with the boy and were touched that a child would choose items for his family and not himself. The real sin, they felt, was that little children lived in homes that lacked basic necessities like soap and toilet paper.

But a few reacted to the story with indignation. "Life is not a free ride. I hope he was punished for stealing," said one. "I hope he was made aware that actions have consequences, and he can't get away with this in life," said another.

So what do you think? Whose toilet paper is it?

𝓡

· ·

Random Acts

The great souls among us have always pointed to kindness as the virtue among virtues. The Dalai Lama said: "My religion is very simple. My religion is kindness." The Talmud teaches that "the beginning and end of Torah is performing loving acts of kindness." And Proverbs reminds us, "You who pursue righteousness and kindness will find life."

For a while there was a big movement in the United States urging people to practice random acts of kindness. A book of that name contained page after page of true stories of simple acts of kindness. Stories of someone giving a one-hundred-dollar tip to a waitress when the total bill was less than twenty dollars; of a New York cab driver giving someone a free ride; of neighbors painting a house for a wheelchair-bound widow.

If I had known they were collecting stories, I would have sent this one:

If you saw him on the street you'd be both frightened and disgusted. He had dirty, stringy hair and disheveled, torn clothing. He'd shuffle along, head hanging low, but if he looked up you might be alarmed by the wild look in his eyes. He might even fall on the pavement and go into a seizure. His name was Frank, and he was tormented by alcohol and epilepsy.

Sister Mary Miller, director of our soup kitchen, said that when she took over the kitchen twelve years ago she would often let Frank come in a little early for a cup of coffee. He never spoke. He sipped his coffee in a corner, alone.

One afternoon, when only he and Sister Mary were in the kitchen, a farmer walked in with two enormous beef livers. "Our shelves were bare then and I was grateful for the meat, but I looked at all that liver and began muttering aloud about what I was going to do with it," Sister Mary said.

Then she heard Frank mumble something. "What did you say?" Sister Mary asked.

"I used to be a butcher," Frank stammered.

"Well, what are you waiting for," she said. "Wash up and get busy."

For the rest of the afternoon and all the next morning Frank worked like a surgeon, carefully removing the thin membrane and carving steak-size pieces of liver. He and Sister Mary had a wonderful animated conversation the entire time.

But when the work was done, so was Frank. For the next twelve years, he barely said hello to Sister Mary. Often she would cradle his head and stroke his hand when he had a bad seizure at the kitchen, but they never talked again. "Others might see me holding Frank's head and be repulsed," Sister Mary said, "but all I could see was the good heart. All I could remember was the beef liver and his loving kindness to me."

Sister Mary was devastated when Frank, along with three other drifters, burned to death in a local hotel. But she is sure God practiced a random act of kindness and just threw open the gates for Frank.

Relationships

Thomas Merton wrote:

Do not depend on the hope of results. When you are doing the sort of work you have taken on, you may have to face the fact that your work will be apparently worthless and even achieve no result at all, if not perhaps results opposite of what you expect. . . . Gradually you struggle less and less for an idea and more and more for specific people. In the end it is the reality of personal relationships that saves everything.

As Merton knew so well, work for peace and justice among the poor is heartbreaking. You can gear your life to a gospel ideal like equal distribution of goods and find that despite your best efforts the gap between rich and poor continues to widen. Meanwhile, your hair has turned gray and the temptation to quit grows stronger.

Eventually you stand at a crossroads: discouraged by corporate greed, beaten down by government hypocrisy and deceit, numbed by human apathy, sickened by church politics, weary of empty rhetoric, mindful of your own inadequacy and sinfulness, sometimes even betrayed by the people you thought were walking with you. So why stay in the struggle?

Because of a few people you met along the way, perhaps. The relationships I forged in my visits to Haiti keep the flame burning, however low, in my heart.

I have no faith in a grand political theory that will bring justice to the poor, but I'm committed to Claudette Werleigh, my friend, who works tirelessly and fearlessly for a better Haiti.

I have no hope that the institutional church will ever confront the powerful and stand with the poor and defenseless, but I'm committed to the ideals of ousted president Jean-Bertrand Aristide, my friend, who ignited a country by enfleshing the gospel.

I have no proof that my small efforts will ever change the system of injustice, but I'm committed to little Elifet, my friend, who begged me for medicine in Port-au-Prince so that he could live another week.

In the end, it's my friendship with people like Claudette and Aristide and Elifet that save everything. Or at least save me from abandoning the struggle for justice.

Resilience

Last evening Mary and I were taking a walk for an ice cream cone and we met a family from the soup kitchen. The wife had just had a gall-bladder operation at a local hospital and was walking home—IV bandages still on her arm. We were incredulous. "You're walking fifteen blocks after an operation! Why didn't you get a cab?" Mary asked. "Oh, there was some mixup and we had to walk," the husband said, shrugging his shoulders in that resigned way that the poor adopt when confronted with those situations they consider their lot in life. "We'll be okay." And on they walked.

Like this couple, the inner-city neighbors who pass my front stoop each day are a collage of resilience, perseverance, and profound hope. To experience only the tip of their tragic stories would lock most of us into the gray cell of despair. Yet they still rise each dawn and listen to what poet Czeslaw Milosz in "On Angels" calls the angel's voice:

Day draws near
another one
do what you can.

Saviors

I don't know about you, but I've been saved many times in my life. There was a teacher who saved me from taking the wrong direction. A parent who saved me from poor life choices. A friend who saved me from myself.

These are saviors in ordinary time. There are also extraordinary or high-feast saviors. People who actually risk their lives to save others. One of my favorite saviors is Benedictine sister Maria Mikulska. She risked her life to save human beings in Nazi-occupied Poland during World War II.

One of the young Jewish boys that she helped save grew up to be the internationally renowned artist Samuel Bak. In a moving memoir he writes how his mother and he, at age seven, were smuggled into the convent cloister and he met his savior, Sister Maria. "One of the nun's hands touched my hair and rested itself gently on my head. I looked up. . . . A smiling face that looked at me with tenderness. It had a perfectly round shape, a most healthy skin, and was beautifully framed in the white starched construction. Its age seemed undetermined, its goodness unlimited." Sister Maria took seven-year-old Samuel under her wing, and he and his family lived in safety at the convent, for many months.

One day German soldiers surrounded the convent and the sisters hid the Jewish family in the attic. Bak writes, "Very quickly every corridor, every room was occupied by armed men. They evacuated the sisters with incredible brutality and sent them off to labor camp."

Samuel and his family escaped at night and remained free for two years before being captured and sent to a labor camp. Smuggled out of the camp in a sack by his father, Samuel was reunited with his mother, who had also escaped. When police began searching the neighborhood where they were hiding, Samuel's mother grabbed him in her arms and raced along an ancient wall, stopping in front of a small door. Bak recalls: "The banging on the door brought the sound of steps. It was opened by a smallish, bent, seemingly elderly woman, clad in drab, gray working clothes. Her graying hair was showing from under her dark scarf. She took us in and closed the door. Looking at us with gaping, unbelieving eyes, she stretched out her arms and with a yelp in her voice, enclosed us in her embrace. This was Maria Mikulska."

She and a few other sisters had come back from the camp and were working as cleaning women in the convent, which was now headquarters of the Nazi organization that collected archives and documents of conquered territories. All the rooms and corridors were stacked with books and documents. Sister Maria and Father Stakauskas had made a hideaway for a small group of Jews under the books and were providing them with food. "Had the authorities discovered their acts of great humanity," Bak writes, "they would have been tortured and executed. Their courage and devotion went beyond anything I have encountered."

Samuel Bak survived the war thanks to an extraordinary woman, Sister Maria, who saved his life not once, but twice. All around the globe, in our cities, in our neighborhoods, there are children like young Samuel who need saviors. The Talmud teaches, "If you save one life, it is as if you saved the world."

Soup Kitchen

I was there when we opened the soup kitchen in the early 1970s. For the first meal there were thirteen servers and one guest. We shrugged our shoulders and said, "Maybe Erie doesn't need a soup kitchen." Now Emmaus, our soup kitchen, serves almost two hundred people a day.

We were so *idealistic* then. So convinced that our little soup kitchen was a finger in a dike that would soon be repaired. We had such high hopes for a church that in the 1970s was rediscovering its social-justice roots. Statements from the Vatican and national conferences of bishops were announcing that work for justice was a constitutive element of the gospel. To be a follower of Jesus, in other words, meant changing structures that caused hunger and poverty. The guiding light for all gospel actions was to be a preferential option for the poor.

We believed that with enough teaching the words of Saint Basil would be understood and implemented: "The bread in your cupboard belongs to the hungry person; the coat hanging unused in your closet belongs to the one who needs it; the shoes rotting in your closet belong to the person who has no shoes; the money which you put in the bank belongs to the poor. You do wrong to everyone you could help, but fail to help."

Decades later we are still standing at the dike trying to hold back the surging waters of hunger and poverty. It would be such a gift to the poor to announce that Emmaus is closing because it is no longer needed. Instead, in our third decade of sharing bread, we opened a soup kitchen for children, euphemistically called Kids' Cafe.

Why are we doing this? I could list hunger statistics and pleas for an after-school feeding program from inner-city schoolteachers and nurses. I could tell you about the 250 Kids' Cafes around the country. Instead, let's remember the inner-city child who got a scholarship to our summer camp and reported: "Guess what? They eat three times a day here."

How many children are there in this, the richest country the civilized world has ever known, who do not realize that three meals a day is a norm? What do these hungry children bode for the future of our society?

Surprise

Here is one of my all-time favorite stories: A certain poet mystic was respected for his piety and virtue. Whenever anyone asked him how he had become so holy, he always answered, "I know what is in my Bible." One day a new disciple innocently asked, "Well, what is in the Bible?" "In the Bible," said the mystic, "there are two pressed flowers and a letter from my friend Jonathan."

Isn't that a great story? I mean, what a surprise ending. Who expects flowers and a letter from a friend to be the answer? The holy man's response just wreaks havoc with all the "right" and "true" answers that we have stored in our heads. Answers we spew out with the certainty of a chief justice. Maybe I should put more effort into listening to stories. Especially stories that surprise, that shatter my stereotypes and blast gaping holes in my certainties.

Stories like these: Sister Claire, a worker at our soup kitchen, arrived at Tom's house and honked the horn. She wanted him to help deliver a truckload of furniture. Most of his adult life, Tom has been on Supplemental Security Income, often homeless and hungry. Chances are that if you ran into Tom on the street in the evening, you'd be a little nervous. Sometimes he looks wild. Determined to get off government assistance, he is just starting to earn a little money doing maintenance work at the pantry and the Art House. Tom came to the front door and motioned for Sister Claire to get out. "I want to show you my garden," he said. Sister Claire went with him to the backyard and admired his small plot of zucchini and tomatoes and peppers. Then Tom picked the ripest tomato and largest zucchini and handed them to her. "These are for the soup kitchen," he said. "The Bible says we are to offer the first fruits back to God." Surprise!

Speaking of the Neighborhood Art House, what class do you think the inner-city boys like best? Well, if you saw the list of offerings, you might guess Kung Fu. You might guess that, but you'd be wrong. The most popular class is flower arrangement. Surprise. The boys, as well as the girls, love handling fresh flowers, different varieties each day, and forming them into bouquets. They love taking the roses and gladioli and tiger lilies and orchids home each day. "This is the first time we ever had real flowers in my house," one of the boys told Joe Wieczorek, the local florist who donated the flowers and taught the course.

So next time you're ready to give a "right" answer about the poor, remember Tom's tomato and zucchini and the inner-city toughs arranging roses. Those would be two good stories to put in your bible.

𝒯
· ·

Theology

It was closing time at the soup kitchen, and a college student volunteer was clearing and washing the tables, one of the more unpleasant jobs around. Sister Mary Miller, the director of the soup kitchen, walked over to help the girl wipe up spilled coffee, bread crumbs, and other garbage. "Sure are a lot of dirty tables in this joint, aren't there, Nancy," she joked. Before the teenager had a chance to respond, a voice answered, "This ain't a joint, Sister. This is a church."

Sister Mary turned around, a bit startled—she thought everyone had left—and spotted one of the guests tucked in the corner, finishing his dessert. She walked over and sat down at his table. "Why did you say that, Joe? Why do you think this is a church?"

Joe looked at her and said simply: "Because this is where I find God, Sister Mary. This is where God's work is done."

I like this story because it illustrates once again that the best theology is not necessarily found in thick volumes on library shelves or in high-powered seminars on religion. No, the best theology—our feeble attempts to understand who or what God is—often come from the mouths of the poor.

Joe knows a church when he's in one. The Emmaus community is the dwelling place, the house of God in his life.

Eleven-year-old Amanda and her five-year-old niece know it too. One New Year's Day Amanda called the soup kitchen and said: "Sister Mary, we have no food. Can I come down?"

"Of course I said yes," explains Sister Mary, "but I had no idea of the distance." The two girls walked seventeen blocks in freezing weather, arriving at the kitchen chilled to the bone, with red ears and cheeks, with noses dripping from the cold.

"I didn't know whether to scold them for walking such a distance or hug them to take away the shivers," says Sister Mary. "I pulled both of them into my arms and asked, 'Why did you walk so far?'"

Little Amanda explained, "I remembered that you said if we ever needed help, if we ever needed anything, we should call you. We need help."

So Sister Mary packed take-out dinners of pork, sauerkraut, mashed potatoes—the works. She filled a bag with groceries for the rest of the week and drove the two girls home to where Amanda's mother and two other children were waiting. She wished them all a Happy New Year.

What is the church? The poor offer these definitions. The church is where God's work is done. The church is where you call if you ever need help, and help is given.

Tithing

Her unspoken question hung over the crowd like the Good Friday clouds gathering in the sky: What will you do about this injustice?

The woman was speaking at the annual Good Friday pilgrimage sponsored by the Benedictine Sisters of Erie. The seven-mile walk winds from the downtown Cathedral to the monastery, with participants stopping along the route to pray at contemporary stations of the cross.

One of the stops this year was at a women's knitting project started by our soup kitchen. At the station a single mother who had been through the program testified how the project taught her work skills that enabled her to apply for a job at a large supermarket chain. She talked about being hired part-time with no benefits and how the company refused to give full-time work to 70 percent of its workers. She talked about having to take a second part-time job cleaning offices three times a week so she could care for her four boys. While she read her statement, every part of her body trembled, but she didn't break down. That she got through her testimony was the best proof of someone beginning to stand on her own two feet. When she finished, every person on the pilgrimage was weeping, including myself. Part of me was grateful that I could still cry over life's lousy injustices, that my heart was not totally jaded.

Yet her question lingered: What will you do about this injustice?

I once heard a speaker address this question and suggest three responses. The speaker told us to respond to injustice by educating ourselves and others about the root causes of injustice, to work for legislative change, and to tithe our time by working with the poor.

It was the tithing of time that stayed with me. Tithing is an honored religious discipline usually associated with money. To tithe means giving one-tenth of what you earn back to God. The speaker was asking us to give one-tenth of our working time to the God who lives in the poor. That equals about four hours a week in a homeless shelter, a prison, a soup kitchen, a food bank, or any place the poor gather.

Tithing time, I think, will have the greatest impact on righting injustice. Why? Because if we commit ourselves to poor people, we will get to know them. By tithing our time with the poor, we will hear a story or two and the stories will change us. Statistics on hunger, poverty, the ravages of war will now wear a human face. We will get to know nine-year-old Tyshana at the after-school reading program and get angry when we find out that she doesn't eat supper at the end of the month because her mother's food stamps are gone. We will go to a women's shelter and befriend Lisa, a battered woman, and be filled with rage when we learn that she returned to her abusive boyfriend because her checks stopped and she has no money. We will meet Lee, a veteran, in a homeless shelter and listen to his horror stories of war and realize he will never again function in society, that he will always need shelters and halfway houses.

I know this because one of the main reasons that I was crying over the woman's testimony on Good Friday was that I know her story. I know her heartbreaking personal history. I took her children to Little League; I am godmother to one of her boys. I realized, too, that my tears of compassion were mingled with tears of rage. I wanted to tear down with my bare hands the system that sentenced her to bare survival.

Will tithing time bring justice to the poor? It depends on how closely we listen to the stories. Only one-tenth of the work week, but imagine the change in society if tithing fills enough of us with holy rage.

Tony

Tony hangs out. On street corners, in bars, on stoops, in soup-kitchen lines. Black, no skills, no job. One of those able-bodied men that give true God-fearing Americans every reason to point the finger and accuse, "lazy, welfare cheat."

But those finger-pointers don't see Tony at the soup kitchen. No job is too menial for Tony. He cleans the soiled toilets, mops the drunks' vomit, wraps the garbage. You can count on Tony to lift the heavy buckets of soup and carry the boxes loaded with canned goods. Every night he sweeps and scrubs the floor. "Anything else you want me to do, Sister Mary?" is Tony's mantra.

Last Christmas, Tony asked Sister Mary, a potter, how much one of her mugs costs. "I don't have much money, but I want to buy one," he said.

"Why do you want it?" Sister Mary asked.

"To give away," Tony explained. "Every Christmas I try to give at least one present to someone who's been good to me just so I remember it's Christmas."

Treasure Box

Once upon a time some disciples were finishing their training with the Master. As one of the disciples was preparing to leave for home, the Master presented her with a box. "I am going to give you this gift, my daughter, but you must promise me that you will keep the condition of the gift. It is a very ancient tradition. Everyone who has ever owned this box has kept the tradition." And the Master placed in her hand a small, hand-carved, wooden box.

The disciple said, "I promise you, Master, that I will keep the condition. What is it?" And the Master said, "Wherever you place this little box, it must always face east."

So the disciple went home and put the little box in her living room, facing east. But when she did, suddenly, the entire room no longer seemed "to work." It was out of harmony, out of balance. So she had to redecorate the living room completely. But then she noticed that the rest of the house did not match the living room. So she had to completely redecorate and change the entire house. Then she looked out of the window and saw that the garden no longer fit her house.

Frustrated, she sat down and wrote the Master a letter. "Dear Master," she said, "the little box you gave me is dangerous! I have had to change and redecorate my living room, and then my house, and now, I know, my garden. I can easily guess what is next—the neighborhood, and then. . . . "

I like to think that the treasure box is prayer, that if we pray in the right spirit, if we, in other words, face east, pray as God wants us to pray, then we will find ourselves changing.

I am convinced that most of the time I have placed my treasure box in the west or hidden it in the southern corner of my heart. If I really prayed, if I were facing east, then surely I would find myself more out of harmony with the status quo.

I say I pray, yet two-thirds of the world's children will go to bed hungry tonight and that will not disturb my sleep. I say I pray, yet women are still second-class citizens in the church—

excluded from any decision making—and yet I have not consistently confronted church leadership. I say I pray, yet millions in Africa, mostly women and children, are dying a torturous death due to AIDS and I do little to pressure my government to change its policies.

If I were truly praying, I would see how off center, how out of harmony, my community, my neighborhood, my country, my world are with the God of love. And I would do something about it. True prayer should, as the scripture says, turn our hearts of stone to hearts of flesh. True prayer, in other words, is a box facing east; it changes us. It changes how we see God, how we see ourselves, how we see our brothers and sisters around the world, how we see all creation. True prayer radically shifts our lives.

U

Undeserving Poor

The woman was livid, pounding her fist on the table. "I wouldn't give a cent to those soup-kitchen bums," she declared. "They spend my tax money on whiskey and cigarettes. They have children just to get bigger welfare checks. They're probably too lazy to get jobs. They don't deserve a free meal."

Ah, the undeserving poor. How often we've heard those tirades.

But let's pretend for a minute that the woman's accusations are true. Let's say that those who eat at soup kitchens spend their meager checks on booze and drugs instead of food and shelter. Let's agree that they are all offered jobs and refuse them because they are lazy. Let's agree that they only have children because they want more government money.

Would that make them less deserving of help? Any less deserving than we are? It depends on whether you look at it through Wall Street's eyes or Jesus' eyes, I guess.

"We love," suggests 1 John 4:19, "because God first loved us." That love comes through in one of my favorite Hasidic tales. According to the tale, the rabbi of Sassov once gave the last money in his pocket to a man of ill repute. When his disciples objected, he asked, "Shall I be more finicky than God, who gave it to me?"

None of us deserves what we have. All of us are recipients of an unconditional love, poured out and overflowing.

Creation itself is a gift given without human effort. Who among us deserves another minute of life? Who among us deserves forgiveness for the hurt and harm we have scattered like sand on a seashore? A child's love, the smell of coffee in the morning, a slice of freshly baked bread, a brilliant sunset—everything and everyone is a gift.

Each of us stands before God as a beggar, totally dependent on God's sustaining love. All we are asked to do is to imitate God: to give without judgment or label, to give because we are *all* "undeserving poor."

Daily we receive a torrent, a flood of undeserved gifts from the unending waterfall of God's goodness. And daily we are given opportunities to imitate the torrent through acts of kindness and unconditional love.

Voices of Haiti

A priest begged us, "When you leave Haiti, please remember the voices you heard here." And these are the words that haunt my dreams:

"We don't want to be rich," the peasant woman pleaded. "We only want not to be poor."

"Why are the dogs so thin?" someone asked the guide. "They are thin because the people eat the garbage," was the answer.

"Women are used as brooms," explained the young feminist organizer. "Used and then thrown in the corner."

The political analyst instructed: "This is the attitude of the powerful toward our nation: Some countries have no reason to exist. They should be dropped in the ocean. One is Haiti."

"Haiti? It's like we're lying on a hospital bed in a coma but are still able to hear," said the bishop. "Gathered around the bedside, people are discussing us as if we were already dead. But Haiti is not a corpse and resents being treated as one."

The peace activist was passionate: "Tell our friends in the United States not to forget us. As long as we know there are people who stand with us, we can go on."

"*J'ai faim*. I am hungry," said the old woman, lifting her dress to show an infection. "*J'ai faim*. I am hungry," pleaded the young boy pressing his face against the window of our locked van and following us for blocks through Port-au-Prince traffic. "*J'ai faim*. I am hungry," the child begged, tugging at my skirt and pointing silently to her swollen stomach and her mouth. *"J'ai faim.* I am hungry. I am hungry."

"Please listen to the voices you heard in Haiti," the priest begged us. "Listen to the voices and follow your conscience."

Vow of Nonviolence

A group of political activists were attempting to show the Master how their ideology would change the world. After listening very carefully, the Master replied, "An ideology is as good or as bad as the people who make use of it. If a million wolves were to organize for justice, would they cease to be a million wolves?"

Or, as Saint Francis put it, "While you are proclaiming peace with your lips, be careful to have it even more fully in your heart."

It's for this reason—to have heart match word—that I took a vow of nonviolence. I took the vow in the Nevada desert on August 6, 1985, the fortieth anniversary of the bombing of Hiroshima.

To take a public vow of nonviolence in a desert—any desert—is a bold and blatant confrontation with the forces of evil lurking within us. All is stripped to zero. But to proclaim the nonviolent message of Jesus in this desert was to tempt and test—perhaps beyond endurance—the potency of the Principalities and Powers. In this desert dwelt the heart of darkness. In this desert was the Nevada nuclear-weapons test site. Here all United States nuclear-test explosions occur. Here an announced test took place every three weeks.

Months before, the religious peace community, including the Catholic peace movement, Pax Christi USA, had issued a call to come here on the anniversary of the birth of the atomic age to demand an end to nuclear testing.

We left Las Vegas in the pre-dawn hours and drove sixty-five miles to the test-site entrance. Ninety of us then processed single file—a long space between each—for two miles through the desert to Camp Desert Rock, one mile from the main gate.

The silent walk was a new experience in solitude—nothing but cactus; brush; relentless sun; wide, wide skies; and me. It was impressive in a terrifying way.

Gleaned from the acres of sand was a deeper understanding of insignificance coupled with a deeper awareness of the abiding presence of God. I prayed a line from Thomas à Kempis in a new way: "Enlarge thou me in love, that with the inward palate of my heart I may taste how sweet it is to love, and to be dissolved, and as it were to bathe myself in thy love." Was it possible to love as limitlessly, as unrelentingly as the God of the desert?

When we arrived at Camp Desert Rock, Anne McCarthy, a new postulant in our Benedictine community, and I stepped aside from the group, joined hands, and recited a vow of nonviolence.

As part of a national action commemorating the bombing of Hiroshima and Nagasaki, Pax Christi USA had invited Christians to take a vow of nonviolence for one year. All across the country people were signaling their total break with violence.

Taking the vow was not a proclamation that we were nonviolent. Rather, the public pledge signaled a decision, a conscious commitment to allow nonviolence to permeate all phases of our lives. "A journey of a thousand miles begins with one step," observed Confucius. The vow of nonviolence is a small step, but a step nonetheless, toward a nonviolent heart.

For Anne and me, the setting of our vow was particularly meaningful. Everywhere we could feel our monastic ancestors. All the ancient desert fathers and mothers who had protested the linkage of church and state and said no to militarism were present. All of the members of our monastic family, who carried the nonmilitary tradition in the early church, came to witness. Abba Anthony was sitting on a rock. Pachomius peered out of a cave. Syncletica gave her blessing. Martin of Tours smiled.

We proclaimed our vow: "Recognizing the violence in my own heart, yet trusting in the goodness and mercy of God, I vow for one year to practice the nonviolence of Jesus by actively resisting evil and working nonviolently to abolish war and the causes of war from my own heart and from the face of the earth."

A simple no to death. Yet one felt the tremors beneath the scorching sands, the gods of war thrashing wildly in sleep, nightmares beyond imagining.

Seven of us, representing the sponsoring groups, joined hands and stretched across the highway. At 8:16 a.m., the exact time the first nuclear bomb turned Hiroshima to ashes, we stepped across the no-trespassing line, knelt down and were arrested. A fitting first action for a vow of nonviolence, the thirty-six hours in jail a mini-retreat to ponder its implications and possibilities.

Vow of Nonviolence Continued

An old Hasidic rabbi would cross the village square each morning on his way to the temple to pray. One morning a large Cossack soldier, who happened by in a vile mood, accosted him, saying, "Hey, Rebby, where are you going?" The old rabbi said, "I don't know." This infuriated the Cossack. "What do you mean you don't know? Every morning for twenty-five years you've crossed the village square and gone to the temple to pray. Don't fool with me. Who do you think you are, telling me you don't know?" He grabbed the old rabbi by the coat and dragged him off to jail. Just as he was about to push him into the cell, the rabbi turned to him saying, "You see, I didn't know."

Five years after taking the Pax Christi vow of nonviolence, I find this Hassidic tale a good way to explain where the vow has taken me. In fact, the story speaks to vow takers of all kinds—married, religious, private, or public. What vow taker really knows where he or she is going? Really?

Oh, some project a clear goal and imagine themselves walking toward it, but that illusion is soon shattered. How many, I wonder, took the vow of nonviolence and steeled themselves for a lifestyle of long fasts, solidarity with the poor, civil disobedience, and feared they didn't have the mettle to meet this self-spun scenario?

And how many discovered that they could have spared themselves the agony? Bread-and-water fasts, rubbing shoulders with the poor, even prison cells are easy. A vow of nonviolence makes tougher demands. It forces the vow taker to stand in front of a mirror. And that's not always a pleasant experience.

Once I attended a prayer workshop where we were encouraged to take a picture of something in life that was difficult for us to deal with, but which we had come to value—and then to carry that picture in our wallets. That's easy, I thought. I always carry it with me. It's the photo on my driver's license. Nothing is more difficult for me to deal with than myself, but over the years I certainly have come to love myself.

The vow forces us to focus on the violence hidden in our hearts that now flashes like a neon sign on Times Square: the raging anger in me that explodes when my positions are questioned . . . driving through city traffic on a very short fuse . . . discovering that my enemy is the bishop and I can't tolerate him. "Instead of hating all the people you think are warmongers, hate the appetites and disorders in your own soul which are the causes of war," Thomas Merton wrote.

Such epiphanies mean the vow is working. Ask any good vow taker and he or she will tell you that faithfulness led to self-knowledge. The trick is not to panic once violent feelings and actions surface—God, I am not worthy to be a peacemaker. The point of the vow is not to become scrupulous or guilt-ridden. Rather, the purpose of the vow is to lead beyond self-knowledge to reach self-acceptance.

There is a story about a man who took great pride in his lawn, only to wake up one day and find a large crop of dandelions. He tried every method he knew to get rid of them. Still they plagued him. Finally, he wrote the Department of Agriculture. He enumerated all the things he had tried and closed his letter with the question, "What shall I do now?" In a few weeks the reply came: "We suggest you learn to love them."

To learn to love all the dandelions that live in me is spiritual maturity. It's only when I can say yes to myself as I am that

God can work in me. Otherwise, I'm too busy trying to make myself better than God made me. And I get in God's way.

To say yes to myself might mean that, if I accept the weaknesses in myself, I can accept the weaknesses in others more easily. So there is no need to be so defensive, no need to project my deepest fears about myself onto the enemy.

To say yes to myself and my life might even mean that I rejoice in who I am, in my existence as it is. Paul Tillich laid out life's greatest challenge: "Simply accept the fact that you are accepted." But how difficult it is to believe that outrageously beautiful fact.

Waiting

When I take my friend Zelda to the welfare office, I know I'm in for a long wait. I try not to think about the hours spent there as a waste of time, but I find myself anxious to be about other projects. I get antsy and keep glancing at my watch, never fully present to Zelda, the book I'm flipping through, or the other people around me.

If, at the end of the day, someone asks me what I did today, I reply without hesitation, and with a touch of resentment: "Absolutely nothing. I spent all afternoon waiting with Zelda." Immediately my words bounce back and confront me with a tough question: Do I really believe waiting is useless? Or am I avoiding the harsh truth that I don't know how to wait?

Years ago I had the opportunity to engage in two exhausting bouts with waiting. In the first, I participated in a pray-in at the White House and spent about twenty-eight hours in the DC jail, almost all of it in waiting, just waiting. I never expected the waiting to bother me as it did. It shocked me that I couldn't be at ease with the present moment, I who pride myself on a love of solitude and often romanticize the jail cell as the next best thing to a hermitage. Twenty-eight hours without a book or a typewriter, and I was raging inside with quiet desperation. It was as if the gray prison walls had begun to seep through my pores and settle inside me. All my words and actions for peace seemed futile and senseless and empty. I couldn't pray or concentrate; I could merely struggle to maintain an inner calm. Many nights since then I have drifted into an uneasy sleep wondering—am I that shallow? Are my spiritual resources that thin?

And I waited for my mother to die this year. Although it took less than a week, it was not an easy death. The doctor thought she had a severe asthma attack, and when I went to the hospital, I found her on a respirator, a trapped animal, squirming, fighting like hell to break free. Although her arms were strapped, she managed to scribble two notes on a pad beside her bed. What turned out to be her final words to me were: "I have been committed here against my will," and "I want to go home."

I grabbed her hand and tried to reassure her: "Mom, you're doing better today. Try to relax. The machine is going to help you." But she shook her head no over and over again. The look in her eyes screamed what she couldn't say, "I am dying, Mary Lou. Help me."

How could I help her? Oh, I sat and held her hand, and when she slipped into a coma, I recited prayers aloud and tried to keep up a conversation on the chance she could still hear. But the vigil I kept was not expectant. I was waiting for nothing. Even the poignant childhood memories that surged upon me as I sat by the bedside were infected by a sense of absurdity. Behold the woman who bore thee and on whose breasts you sucked—see her kidneys collapse, see her blood pressure plunge, see her heart stop.

Both of these standoffs with waiting have frightened me a bit. In jail I discovered I had little to wait with, and my mother's death forced me to deal with the essential question of whether there is anything worth waiting for.

Walking 1

"How much money do you have pledged," my brother Ed asked.

"About one thousand dollars," I answered.

"You can make more than that in one good tag day," said. "Why kill yourself walking from Pittsburgh to Erie?"

He's right, of course. But money is not the only reason why I took part in a long-distance walk organized by CROP, the community hunger appeal of Church World Services. CROP takes as its motto, "We walk because they walk." Supposedly one can identify more closely with a refugee after completing a 155–mile walk.

It was a grueling experience. There were pulled groin muscles, swollen tendons, aching muscles, sunburn, and blisters galore shared by our group of twelve. And these resulted in minor acts of heroism.

Two in our group were hobbling by the end of the second day with pulled muscles and large blisters on their feet, but they continued on sheer willpower for five more days before accepting a ride in Meadville.

Had we been walking in the drought regions of Africa, of course, these two might have been left to die on the road. So you get some idea of what it's like to be part of a caravan, tired and hungry, walking on and on. And I gained a little insight into the kind of self-discipline needed to survive an ordeal.

Which brings me back to my brother's question. Why walk 155 miles? Here's why.

After a big demonstration in Washington, I was returning to Erie in a bus filled mostly with college kids. The protest had been Saturday afternoon, and the kids apparently had been entertained that evening with rock concerts that featured plenty of alcohol and drugs.

It was no surprise that on Sunday afternoon the whole bus was passed out—kids sleeping on the floor, in the john, everywhere. I had had a good night's sleep, so I began reading *One Day in the Life of Ivan Denisovich* by Alexander Solzhenitsyn.

Here I was reading this story of one man's heroic struggle to survive in a concentration camp in the middle of snoring, sprawling, hung-over protesters, a group that thought it was an army for justice. I was tempted to nudge awake the kid next to me and say, "You know it's going to take a lot more than this to bring about the kind of world we all marched for

rday—one with no starving children. It's going to take
ople with the inner resources of Ivan Denisovich.
So I took a 155-mile walk.

Walking 2

I have a walking master. His name is Isaiah, the prophet
and peacemaker. Isaiah walked naked and barefoot for three
years through the city of Jerusalem. His walk was a symbolic
action. He walked to shock the people, to teach them a lesson.
It was his way of stating a warning: "Don't participate in military action against Assyria or you will meet with humiliation,
with disaster." The action worked. The people of Jerusalem
did not join forces against Assyria, and the city was spared.

But what a price Isaiah must have paid. It doesn't take much
imagination. Just recall any peace action. Maybe handing out
leaflets at a federal building . . . remember the hostile stares?
Or joining a peace demonstration in Washington, DC . . . remember the accusatory questions? Or committing civil disobedience . . . remember the loss of reputation?

Now, imagine Isaiah walking naked and barefoot for three
years. Not difficult, is it, to feel the ridicule and rejection that
he must have experienced? And yet, my teacher, Isaiah, came
to the end of his three-year pilgrimage and proclaimed, "How
beautiful upon the mountains are the feet of those who bring
glad tidings, announcing peace, bearing good news."

Isaiah has taught me that walking is revolutionary. He has
taught me that people on their feet, walking toward a goal,
can topple empires, can create a taste of the Promised Land.

Think of Gandhi's salt march—the small cadre that swelled
into a national nonviolent army, marching for freedom. "How
beautiful upon the mountains are the feet of those who bring
glad tidings, announcing peace, bearing good news."

Remember the euphoric though short-lived triumph of
Solidarity in Poland, with Lech Walesa carried on the shoulders of the working poor, the throngs singing in the city streets?

"How beautiful upon the mountains are the feet of those bring glad tidings, announcing peace, bearing good news.

Recall the day of victory for the poor in Nicaragua when Somoza was overthrown? Hear the church bells ringing, see the people embracing and dancing in the streets. "How beautiful upon the mountains are the feet of those who bring glad tidings, announcing peace, bearing good news."

Think of the days prior to the Iraq War. Millions of people in the streets around the world, walking together against war, joining voices in a song for peace. "How beautiful upon the mountains are the feet of those who bring glad tidings, announcing peace, bearing good news."

But tomorrow the new government begins to become corrupt, or in time the "little people" are crushed again. Or despite millions of people for peace nothing changes. It only worsens. That may be right. But the moment of hope can never be extinguished. For one second in time everyone has a taste of new beginning, new possibilities, new life. For a brief time the reign of God is present on earth. And who knows? In the 1960s a popular song belted out the promise: "There's a new world coming, and it's just around the bend." We walkers know that "around the bend" is always a surprise. There is only one way to find out—keep walking.

Xerox Monks

Looking for a parable on the state of contemporary monasticism in this country? Embedded in my mind is an old Xerox TV ad in which a short, fat monk performs the "miracle" of finding a duplicating machine to copy in record time all the materials requested by his abbot.

The image of monasticism is still attached to a false romanticism, captured in the ad by strains of Gregorian chant, pealing bells, long robes, and work by candlelight. The romantic is kept in balance by pointing out that monks have indeed adapted to the modern age. Like the majority of Americans, monastics have greeted with open arms all that technology has to offer, blessing it as good—Xerox machines rather than hand-crafted letters being just one example. But the worst indictment is saved for the end—we all smile at the pudgy little monk who gazes pie-eyed toward the heavens and say, "Isn't he cute." I see all of America patting monastery after monastery, convent after convent on the head and saying, "Aren't they nice?" No need to take monasticism seriously; it threatens no person or institution.

Monastic orders are notorious for promoting the idea that sanctity depends on separation from the world, on being different from other human beings. Pictures of hooded figures strolling through the woods and gazing at streams probably have helped sell countless books and records, but they have also reinforced the idea that holiness and peace are found by

fleeing the evil world. Bishop Thomas Gumbleton struck r.
when he said, "It's too easy for monks to be apart from t
world and therefore untouched by the world and consequently
unable to touch the world either."

The irony is that while monastics have tried to project a
"beyond the world" spirituality, they have been as eager as
the rest of the world to grasp and accumulate all that the
American dream has to offer. What started out as a counter-
culture revolution now mirrors the society to a grotesque
degree. We've bought it all: bigger is better and so is having
more; the United States is light to the world; any techno-
logical innovation is progress; capitalism is next to godliness.
And, yes, nuclear weapons make sure that God stays on our
side.

Monastics aren't blatant about these things; like the rest of
middle-class America, they just fit in. That's the horror. Who
these days would equate monasticism with a resistance movement? But that's what it once was.

Anthony, Martin of Tours, Benedict of Nursia, and other
great monastic figures stood as question marks to the values
of their culture. Their positions on the linkage of church and
state, injustice, oppression of the poor, accumulation of wealth,
and violence may not have been popular, but at least their lives
were taken seriously. Now people visit the monasteries "to
get away from it all," to buy cheese and holy cards, to hear
nice singing, and to sell Xerox machines.

I'm not being completely fair. Monasteries do serve as an
oasis for people, constant reminders that silence, solitude, and
prayer are essential for peace of heart and effective ministry.
It's also true that monastic communities, like all religious orders, have attempted to renew, to rediscover the spirit of the
founder, and to live the gospel anew for the times. Documents
dealing with contemporary spirituality, social justice, and world
peace have poured out of religious orders, especially among
the women. However, it's mainly the lives of individual religious or small pockets within the larger community that have
been transformed. Most institutions still taste neither hot nor
cold, tempting Jesus to vomit them out of his mouth.

hat effect would it have, for instance, if monastic communities proclaimed publicly that nonviolence is an essential
monastic value? What would it mean if those entering Christian monastic communities were required to take a vow of
nonviolence?

When I asked Bede Griffiths, the Benedictine monk who
lived in an ashram in India, what he thought of the idea, he
wrote:

> I think a nonviolent attitude to life as expressed in the
> Sermon on the Mount should be basic to monastic life
> and could very well be the subject of a vow. It would
> apply to one's attitude to nature, rejecting all violation of
> nature by science and technology, showing a loving con-
> cern for plants and animals as well as for human beings
> and opposing the violence of political and economic struc-
> tures. As I suggested in *Christ in India, ahimsa* (nonvio-
> lence) should be integral to monastic life, extending not
> only to rejection of war and heavy armaments but also to
> heavy industry and nuclear power, seeking to create a
> society of peace with nature and with God.

> I also look forward to the day when convents and monas-
> teries reclaim their ancient role as sanctuaries, safe places for
> those fleeing from the law. Our homes could harbor "crimi-
> nals" who nonviolently break laws to protect life. Those who
> commit civil disobedience to protest the nuclear-arms race,
> conscientious objectors, should find refuge in our monaster-
> ies, and every effort should be made to explain their position
> to the wider public, every risk taken to protect them.

There are deeper, more fundamental questions that need
to be addressed regarding lifestyle and the sacred cows of capitalism and nationalism. Tom Cullinan, a Benedictine monk
and author who founded an experimental community outside
of Liverpool, England, noted:

> Too many groups work at the level of nuclear arms or
> arms sales and not enough ask why it is that wealthy na-

tions need armaments. There's a tie-in between the arms race and our concept of ownership, what it means for a thing to be mine or yours. If I've got things, I have to defend them; if I own things, I have to lock my front door. And it's at this deep level that monastic life ought to be relevant. We ought to say that nothing ever belongs to any of us. We need a new vision of ownership. But we can only say it by doing it, not by merely voicing it.

These ideas are a far cry from the Xerox monk.

Y

Yuletide Carols

The Advent season is especially meaningful this year. The snows are heavy and deep and comforting. It is easy to pray with Isaiah,

> Though your sins be red as crimson,
> I will make them white as wool.

And there is such silence. City noises, encased in yards of white swaddling, are muffled. Cars, concrete sidewalks, and other hard objects lie buried under the soft snow.

We are forced to slow down—walk carefully so we don't slip; drive cautiously so we don't skid. We can spend more time indoors reading, listening to music, and praying. We prepare. For soon, "when the earth is in peaceful silence, and the night is in the midst of its course, your almighty Word, O Lord, will leap down from heaven."

It's easy to get sucked into thinking that this is what Christmas is all about.

Thank God for the soup kitchen. Is there a lonelier place on earth as Christmas nears? The guys start drinking in the middle of the month so that by Christmas week they can't even hear the words "I'll be home for Christmas" blaring on the radio. It's their only defense. We try to make it less sad. But even handing out brightly wrapped socks and scarves and

lotions, or having a party and singing Christmas carol
drinking hot chocolate doesn't ease the heartbreak.

I'm grateful for both experiences—quiet confident joy at
the coming of the Savior, tempered by the harsh reality of
human suffering. Together, they capture a fuller meaning of
Christmas.

Zeal

One of my favorite desert tales goes like this: Abba Lot went to see Abba Joseph and said: "Abba, as much as I am able, I practice a small rule, all the little fasts, some prayer and meditation, and remain quiet. As much as possible I keep my thoughts clean. What else should I do?" The old man stood up and stretched out his hands toward heaven, and his fingers became like torches of flame. And he said, "Why not be turned into fire?"

I love this monastic tale that captures a heart of zeal, of passion. The scripture scene it brings to mind is the cleansing of the Temple. The disciples, after watching Jesus rid the Temple of thieves, describe him with the words of Psalm 19: "Zeal for your house consumes me."

How would it look if I lived this way? If I were so filled with passion about God's house?

Let's begin with being consumed. The other day a friend of mine attended a seminar on drugs. One of the participants asked the workshop leader, a former drug user himself, what it was like to be hooked? What was the attraction?

The seminar leader asked the participants to remember a time in their lives when they were infatuated with someone. He recalled his own story. "I was working at a hospital," he explained, "and there was this nurse. I thought of her constantly. I made every excuse to walk by her desk. At lunch I would stand by the elevator she used, just to see her and—if I was lucky—to have her brush my sleeve when she left and entered the elevator. I lived for that moment. Her face was the first image I saw on waking. I fell asleep fantasizing about her and, oh, the dreams.

"That," he explained, "is what drug addiction is like. You wear it every second; it haunts your thoughts, your words, your actions. It becomes your reason for getting out of bed in the morning, your sole purpose for making it through the day." This is what being consumed means, what being turned into fire can look like.

As the seminar leader's example makes clear, addiction or "being consumed" by drugs, alcohol, power, or another human being can be a dangerous thing, a sickness. But it can also be sanctifying. A saint can be described as one whose life burns away in God's use. "Keep the flame going, but low; burning, but not burning up," Dan Berrigan challenges.

Zeal can be a terrifying word, too. Images of sword-wielding crusaders, fire and brimstone evangelists, fanatics of every shape and cause come to mind. We think of words like *bitter*, *harsh*, *self-righteous*, and *judgmental*. We imagine people who see the world as black and white, who know no mercy for gray in individual lives.

In the cleansing of the Temple, we get another picture of zeal. Here we see that to be filled with zeal is to be absorbed by passion, by fervor, by desire for an ideal. The one afire is centered and focused; all of life points in one direction, and the arrow never wavers.

In the cleansing of the Temple Jesus becomes, as the desert tale describes it, someone who is turned into fire. But what is Jesus afire for? The scripture explains that all Jesus' energy is directed toward God's house, the holy of holies, the place where the sacred dwells. But the temple Jesus is afire for is the human body. "Destroy this temple," he said, "and in three days I will raise it up."

Jesus tells us that it will take the destruction of his own body to create a new sanctuary, a temple of living stone. In the cleansing of the Temple, Jesus smashes the temple of stone and begins to build a temple of flesh. Jesus is being consumed, then, for us. Each human being is a temple of God. As Saint Paul tells us, "Do you not know that your body is a temple of the Holy Spirit within you, given by God?" (1 Cor 6:19).

How would it look if we rekindled the fire inside? Can anyone say of me that zeal for the temple of God consumes me? Am I spending myself, giving my own body in unrelenting service and self-sacrifice for others?

Zeal for the temple of God . . . for the suffering, the poor, the lonely, the sick, for you . . . for you . . . for you. . . . Zeal for the temple of God consumes me.

Zen Wisdom

A Zen monk in Japan wanted to publish the holy books, which at the time were available only in Chinese. The books were to be printed with wood blocks in an edition of seven thousand copies, a tremendous undertaking.

The monk began by traveling and collecting donations for this purpose. A few sympathizers gave him a hundred pieces of gold, but most of the time he received only small coins. After ten years the monk had enough money to begin his task.

But then there was a terrible flood in the area, and famine followed. So the monk took the funds he had collected for the books and spent them to save others from starving. Then he began his work of collecting again.

Fifteen years later an epidemic spread over the country. The monk again gave away what he had collected to help his people.

For a third time he started his work, and after twenty years his wish was fulfilled—the books were printed. The printing blocks that produced the first edition of the holy books can be seen today in a monastery in Kyoto.

The Japanese, however, tell their children that the monk really made three sets of holy books. And, they explain with great pride, the first two invisible sets surpass the third.

This story is a pearl of wisdom for all seekers of truth. First, the Zen monk reminds us to keep our priorities straight. There is always a need for the new, the better, the improved. But any need—no matter how aesthetic or literate or historical or practical—must be measured against the gospel challenge to care first for the poor.

For any person or group to accumulate material things, even much needed and beautiful ones, while ignoring the poor and hungry in its midst, is a clear sign of spiritual decay and decline. On the other hand, the Zen monk speaks loudly about our responsibility to steward and preserve treasures for tomorrow's children. The monk spends his life getting a holy book translated. To build the reign of God on earth as it is in heaven requires a faithful response to two questions. Are the poor our first priority? Are we being responsible stewards of God's treasures—the land, the water, the trees—that will create a kinder future for the generation yet to come?